POST INDEPENDENCE CHAMPUS

DR. S. RANGANATH

Eastern Book Linkers
Delhi : : (India)

Publishers :
Eastern Book Linkers
5825, New Chandrawal,
Jawaharnagar, Delhi-110007
Ph. 3970287

First Edition : 2000

I.S.B.N. : 81-86339-88-4

Type Setting :
Creative Graphics
A-40/6, St. No. 2, Brahmpuri,
Delhi-53 Ph. : 2195643

DEDICATION

This work is dedicated to

Prof. Rajendra Mishra

—Doyen of Modern Sanskrit Literature.

Foreword

Among the various forms of literature adorning Sanskrit (and other Indian languages also in later times) Champu has a remarkable feature. It is a combination of both prose and poetic compositions generally embellished with figures of speech of both sound and sense and affords scope to the poet to show his genius through both the forms and this agreeable combination is rightly compared to the combinations of vocal music and instrumental music हृद्या हि वाद्यकलया कलितेव गीतिः honey and grape juice माध्वीकमृद्वीकयोः सङ्गः when prose and poetic forms are employed so as to suit special occasions and situations the beauty of the combination is enhanced still more. The roots of the Champu are to be found in Vedic Akhyanas and Itihasa puranas and inscriptions. Men of light and learning belonging to both Vedic and Non Vedic religions have made use of this form of literature to portray stories of their traditions as exemplified by Nalachampu and Yasastilakachampu. The five well known Champus and minor champu works of the past have received the attention of scholars.

It is to the credit of the young scholar Dr. S. Ranganath that he has studied and highlighted Champu works of later days also and in this excellent book he has critically analysed Champu works of Sanskrit poets of Post Independence India.

The study of the Champu works depicted in this work removes the misconception that regarding Sanskrit works especially of the champu form, we have merely to gloat over the past. He has analysed the works of even living poets and shows that the above literature and in language embodying it have a continuous and living tradition. His reference to unpublished champu works invites the government and educational bodies to undertake or help their publication.

Dr. Ranganath deserves high appreciation of students of Sanskrit and lovers of our culture for the trouble he has taken in the collection of these works and for his scholarly analysis of them in this book. As in his other works the analysis of facts is crisp and portrayal is simple and beautiful. Having brought out the significant features of works here, he has helped the readers to undertake a detailed study of their beauties and blemishes as Champu works.

May the goddess of learning raise her hand in benediction over this votary of her Samskrita form.

With **Narayana Smaranas**

Bangalore — Sri Sri Rangapriya Sri pāda Sri srih.

Preface

गद्यानुबन्धरसमिश्रित पद्यसूक्तिः
चम्पूप्रबन्धरचना रसना मदीया

Says Bhoja. The import of the definition is that the commingling of prose and poetry is far more appealing than just Prose or poetry independenty of each other. That is the reason why Dandin points out

गद्यपद्यमयीकाचित् चम्पूरित्यभिधीयते।

From these definitions, one can proceed to Venkatadhwari's विश्वगुणादर्शचम्पू and remember the lines सङ्गः कस्य हि न स्वधेत सुधियः माध्वीकमृध्वीकयोः. coming to comparatively recent times Haridasa Bhattacharya points out चम्पयति रसभावादि विशिष्टं वस्तु प्रकशयतीति चम्पूः In the light of these statements and explanations regarding this unique form of Literature it may be recollected that in Sanskrit there is a great tradition of Champu Kavyas as exemplified in the five champus; नलचम्पू of त्रिविक्रमभट्ट, चम्पूरामायण of भोज, चम्पूभारत of अनंतभट्ट, नीलकण्ठविजयचम्पू of नीलकण्ठदीक्षित and विश्वगुणादर्शचम्पू of वेंकटाध्वरी.

In keeping with the continuity of other traditional genres of Sanskrit Literature, the Champu also has been kept alive in the Post Independence Sanskrit Writing. Chief amoung these are

(1) श्री राजरत्नमालाचम्पू of द्विभाषि सोमनाथशास्त्री (1968)

(2) श्री सर्वज्ञेन्द्रचम्पू of गोविन्द भट्ट, (1968)

(3) श्री शरन्नवरात्र चम्पू of कृष्ण जोयिस् (1976)

(4) श्री राघवेन्द्र गुरुसार्वभौम सप्तरात्रोत्सव चम्पू of पंचमुखी राघवेन्द्राचार्य (1977)

(5) श्री विद्यावाचस्पति शम्भुलिङ्गेश्वरविजयचम्पू of पण्डरीनाथाचार्य गलगली (1982)

(6) प्रह्लाद चम्पू of कनराड़ी विट्ठलोपाध्याय (1989)

(7) तीर्थराजचम्पूः of अभिराज राजेन्द्र मिश्र (Published in Various Journals)

(8) अस्मच्चम्पूः of अरेयर् श्रीराम शर्मा (un-published)

These Champu Kavyas present a wide variety of approaches and both qualitatively and quantitatively they represent a massive and impressive contribution to Post Independence Sanskrit Literature. As in the case of my earlier volumes on Drama, Epics and Doota Kavyas the same general pattern is followed in analysing these champus and critical comments are made.

S. Ranganath.

Contents

1

SRI RAJARATNAMALA CHAMPU-DWIBHASHI SOMANATHA SASTRY-1968

Sri Rajaratanamala Champu as the very title indicates is a historical Champu concerned with the life of thirty Shatavahana kings written by Dwibhashi Somanatha Sastry and published by the author from Bhatnavilli, East Godavari District of Andhra Pradesh in the year 1968. The work is divided into nine chapters and each chapter has been termed as Ratna and hence there are Navaratans.Navaratans in Sanskrit Literature has a special significance even from the point of view of one version regarding the life of Kalidasa.In this background, an attempt is made in the following pages to highlight some of the significant points as a sample survey.

The work is dedicated to Sri Kameshwari the Kuladevata of the poet as he himself points out in his Mukhavani;

रचितेऽयं श्रीराजरत्नमालाचम्पूः नः कुलदेवतायै श्रीकामेश्वर्या ऽव समर्पिता।[१]

The special feature of the work is that in all the nine chapters, the first stanza is dedicated to Sri Kameshwari which serves as a constant refrain and can be taken to be Mukuta Style of poems which are popular in Telugu poetry.

यस्यां नासाग्रसुक्ता स्फुरति कुमुदवद्या सरस्याख्येबिम्बे
यस्या व्योमेव तारैर्हरकरनखरैर्लालिता क्रन्लालगीः।
यन्मौलीन्दोरधोंऽसुर्नयति मृगमदस्थासके चन्द्रशोभां
काव्यं चित्रश्रियं मे कलयतु कुलगाऽऽविश्य कामेश्वरी नः॥[२]
(१.१)

त्वत्करकीरेण समं मामनुपाल्योक्ति शिक्षणं कुरुषे।
काव्येऽस्मिन् रचनायाः पूतौ कामेश्वरि त्वमेवासि॥[३]
(२.१)

सदाणाधिपमासने स्थितायां त्वयि पाणं नयनिज स्थिते कुमारे।
उपकृत्य शिरः प्रसारितां तां क्षिप कामेश्वरि मय्यर्पितादीक्षाम्।[४]
(३.१)

अम्ब त्वदीयकृपया रचयामि नूत्नं प्रत्नं मणित्रयमतीत्य
तापत्रयं सुखतरं प्रविलध्य शौरे प्रेम्णेव भक्त उपयाति तुनीयम्॥[५]
(४.१)

श्रीराजच्चरणाम्बुजातविगलन्महात्म्यमाध्वीरसा
साध्वीरानि समग्रनायकमणी राजद्दयावाहिनी।

---

1. Sri Rajaratnamala Champu-Dwibhashi Somanatha Sastry, Bhatnavilli, Prag Godavari Mandalam, 1968, p. 2
2. *Ibid. p.* 3
3. *Ibid. p.* 20
4. *Ibid. p.* 34
5. *Ibid. p.* 47

वाचं सत्कविमोहिनी मम कृतावस्यां रसस्पन्दिनीं
दद्यात्पर्वतनन्दिनी कुलगता कामेश्वरी नस्सदा॥[1] (५.१)

कामेश्वरीं विनाऽऽस्ते का मे दीर्घायुरधिकसुखदात्री।
तामेवती ध्यात्वा षष्ठं रत्नं समारभे सुष्टुम्॥[2]
(६.१)

कामेश्वरी मातृदेवीं मालतीमालिकावतीम्।
मनोन्मनीमहं वन्दे मुनीणमानसहंसिकाम्॥[3] (७.१)

गायत्रीं परदेवीं गायन्तीभिश्च लक्षितां श्रुतिः।
रफायद्दीदितकिरण श्रीयुक्तां भावयामि कामेशीम्[4] (८.१)

नवमं नवमञ्जुभाषणे कुरु रत्नं शुभमूर्ति मत्कृतम्।
अतिलोकंमहत्वभाविते सति! कामेश्वरि वंशदेवते॥[5] (९.१)

ABOUT THE POET

The nineth stanza of the Prathama Ratna gives the family background of the poet;

ब्रह्मज्ञान सुखाब्धि मन्दरगिरिर्येषां महोपज्ञता
जाताऽऽसन्निह वालखिल्यमुनयो ये ब्रह्मवादीश्वराः।
तेषां गोत्रभवो द्विभाष्युपपदः श्रीसोमनाथः कविः॥
पुत्रो "वेंकटरत्न" "बप्प" सुधियोर्यस्तेन यत्नान्मया॥[6]

There was an illustrious family of Valakhilya sages who were Brahmavadins and I am born in that noble family with the Sir name as Dwibhashi and the real name as Somanatha. We may note in passing that even

1. *Ibid. p.* 66
2. *Ibid. p.* 99
3. *Ibid. p.* 112
4. *Ibid. p.* 116
5. *Ibid. p.* 122
6. *Ibid. p.* 2

in Rigveda Samhita we have some Valakhilya hymns which shows the antiquity of the family of the poet.

SUBJECT MATTER

Next, logically subject matter of the work is introduced by the poet;

सम्पूर्णविषया राज्ञा चम्पूस्यान्ध्रभूभुवाम्
रत्नमालाभिधानेन नूत्नमारभ्यते कृतिः॥[1]

The entire work is concerned with the life history of the kings belonging to Andhra province composed with the admixture of prose and poetry.

The style of the poet is dignified and alliteration has suited his descriptions very naturally which could be noted in the following prose passage;

तस्य श्री मुखशातवाहमहाराजस्य आनुवंशिकजनन्या अनन्यशीत-वारि निवारित सातृपालकद्म समुत्क्श्या पुरप्रमोदकपोल पालिकाक्रच-मण्डलन्यस्त शास्त्रकस्तूरिका कुंकुम हारिहारिद्ररेणुमुद्रित तुङ्गतरङ्ग सङ्ग घट्टितपहभङ्गचित्रवर्णा मोद मेदुराम्बसम्भूत पूतपवन पोतपरम्परया तटद्रुमकुसुमाखी हसित लसित कुसुम विसरविसृमर परागपरभागपरीत-परीमल मिलिन्मिलिन्दध्वनिगुम्फित कोकिलाकुहूकुहू कलकलायित कण्ठोपकण्ठया विशालान्द्रभूमि सीमन्तिनी गलान्तिकफलान्तिका चित गौतमीसुवन्तिकया कृता कृत्रिमप्रत्न परिखस्य विलखद्विहाय ससमुन्नताकार गोपुरस्य महीनूपुरस्य तत्पुरस्य पुरसीम्नि रीतिशिला सौध चन्द्रशाला विशालभूभाग भाभासुर महासभा भवननिर्मित मर्म-सिंहासन मधिरुह्य तस्मिन्नरनाथशेखरे विनिर्मल धर्ममूल मनुव्रजन् निजप्रधासन्ततिं स्वसन्ततिमिव पालयति सकलान्ध्रमहनीय महीपुरन्ध्रिका प्रजानांनिर्निर्जितेन्द्रसीरन्ध्रभोग आभोग आसीत्॥[2]

---

1. *Ibid. p.* 2
2. *Ibid. p.* 4

If that is the natural command of the poet over alliteration in prose we can also glean through his mastery of alliteration in poetry here;

कुन्दं सन्ध्ययत्सुगन्धमधुरं मन्दानिलं शर्मणा।
कन्दं कन्द दलयन्मिलिन्दवित्करेः मरिन्दबिन्दूततैः।
तुन्दं बन्धुरयन्मुरव मुखरयत्स्वाध्यायिनामारुणं
बिम्बं बिम्बकदम्बमम्बरतलालम्बं समुद्गुम्फितम्॥[1]

द्वितीयं रत्नम्

Here we have Sri Krishna Shalivahana king deciding to make his nephew named Shatakarni as his successor which resembles the passage of Ayodhya kanda of Champu Ramayana where Dasaratha thinks of coronating his son Rama as his successor;

ईदृग्विद्यमुदारमानसे श्रीकृष्णशालीवाहनमहीपतौ क्षितिं पालयति निर्मलधर्माचार सुन्दरायां तस्यां वसुंधरा यामनीति वर्जनादनीति माप्नुवन्तस्सकलसुखरीतिं तस्य भक्तिप्रतिनुति त्रियामनोरञ्जनाजना बभूवुः। ऽवं स दशवर्षपरिमितं राज्यं कृत्वा सहजपराक्रमक्रमा तुलितकुमारे सहोदरकुमारे गुणकथामृतिस्यन्द सन्दानित प्रजाकर्णे सहोदरकुमारे गुणकथामृतस्यन्द सन्दावित दीक्षाविचक्षणमिव विदित्वातस्य राज्याभिषेचने कैतुकरसासेचनानि लोकलोचनानि सन्तर्पयितुं समृद्दिरमा निरभिवधिमधिरोहयितुं भद्रपीठकां शूभग्रह वीक्षणविलाससमयं कञ्चित्समयं प्रकटीचकार।[2]

When Krishna Shalivahana was ruling Dharmically there was no scope for the entry of adharma and people had great love and regard for him.Having ruled for ten Years he thought of coronating his nephew Sri Shatakarni who was a match to him in every respect.

1. *Ibid. p.* 6
2. *Ibid. p.* 21, 22

With the advent of a new king how the king of Magadha tried to usurp the throne is charmingly described with a beautiful alliteration;

रसाकरे पुष्पकरे बृहद्रथो महीपति साहिधाराजवंशजः।
बभूव राज्यलसभोगलालसः प्रभूतभामानवहावमानसः॥[१]

GRAMMATICAL PROWESS OF THE POET

The famous Vyakarana Sutra "विप्रतिषेधे परं कार्यं" has been beautifully adopted here;

पूर्वापिरकार्यत्वं विप्रतिषेधो यथास्तिशब्दविधौ।
उत्तरदक्षिणभागौ वैदर्भो मागधान्ध्रयोजतौ॥[२]

तृतीय रत्नम्

How under the rule of Shatakarni the glory of Andhras echoed in various directions is nicely portrayed here with an alliteration:—

आन्ध्रेषु स्फुरति ततश्च शातकर्णा
वान्ध्रत्वे दिशिदिशि पुष्पिते यशोभिः।
आन्ध्राणां मृदुमधुरैक मञ्जुवाणी
मञ्जीरध्वनिभिरुदञ्चिते दिगन्ते॥[३]

Even while describing the chief queen's personality;

नागानीकमहेन्द्रसान्द्र धिषणो नागारिसत्वाञ्चितो
नाकौको उद्वाजनिर्जने कऽतिकलानाना विलासार्णवः॥[४]

Next we have the description of the son of Shatakarni, how he was the worthy son of a worthy father;

1. *Ibid. p.* 24
2. *Ibid. p.* 28
3. *Ibid. p.* 34
4. *Ibid. p.* 35

विवर्धमानो द्विजराजनन्दनस्स तु क्रमावाप्त धनुष्कलायणः
धनुर्विदो दोणसमाय तत्पितृसदृगबलौ द्रोणिरिव
व्यराजत धाराधरणपारीणं धराधरसमं धृतौ।
स राजेन्द्रस्सुतं वीक्ष्य करोतिस्म भुवः पतिम्॥[1]

Gradually that prince became a master in archery on par with Drona the expert archer and hence appeared like the son of Drona.

Shatakarni having seen the prowess of his son and thinking him to be capable of shouldering the responsibility of looking after the kingdom wanted to coronate him as his successor.

His son was Mahendraswati. The following description of him

शैशवे कृष्णसंकाशः बाल्ये श्रीरामसन्निभः।
यौवने कल्किकलपर-सन् प्रजामोदमपद्यत॥[2]

(He was like Krishna in his childhood Rama in his boyhood,Kalki in his youth and thus got the affection from his people) resembles the following stanza of Raghuvamsha

शैशवेऽभ्यस्त विद्यानां यौवने विषयैषिणाम्।
वार्धके मुनिवृत्तीनां योगेनांत्ये तनुत्यजाम्॥

चतुर्थं रत्नम्

A fine simili could be noticed in the following stanza where the commond over the different languages of Mahendraswati bereft of Sanskrit is compared to the splendour of the spring in accompaniment of the various flowers but devoid of Malathi;

1. *Ibid. p.* 37
2. *Ibid. p.* 46

स बभौ सर्वभाषाणां सम्पदा संस्कृतं विना।
श्रियेव सर्वपुष्पाणां वसन्तो मालतीं विना॥[1]

A FINE YUGMAKA

The fame of Mahendraswati is nicely portrayed through the following Yugmaka;

कुमार ऽवं सुकुमार धीमरो प्यकल्पयच्छ्री मविकल्पतां पितुः।
यशोभिराशाच यशोभिसद्गुणः पराक्रमेणाऽपि नमत्पराक्रमः॥[2]

The description of the wife of Mahendraswati bears a fine उत्प्रेक्षा :–

विनूत्लरम्भारस गुम्फितान्तरा सिताभ्रमाला नयनानुरञ्जिनी।
स्मरोपनद्धा मणिमेखला रतेर्गभीरशृङ्गार तरङ्गिणी च सा॥[3]

She appeared like a new Rambha,a mass of beautiful white clouds in the clear sky, or like Rati the wife of Manmatha.

During the king's world conquest tour which resembles Chandrapida's world conquest tour in Bana's Kadambari,how he was extended hospitality wherever he went by the womenfulk is nicely depicted by the poet with an alliteration;

काचित्कुम्भस्तनी तन्मृदुपदयुगली मरयशिञ्जञ्जलोधैः
काचिद्भक्त्या लताङ्गी करपुटघटितै रचयामास पुष्पैः।
काचिन्नीलाब्दवेणी व्यजनयतकरा ऽचोलायच्छीतवातान्
काचिद्पद्मानना‌ऽदान्मधरमधु समानीय पानीयमिश्राम्॥[4]

One of the women with heavy bosom washed his tender legs with water, another slendeer lady with

1. *Ibid. p.* 48
2. *Ibid. p.* 48
3. *Ibid. p.* 49
4. *Ibid. p.* 62

utmost devotion offered flowers to him, and still another lady with a long profuse hair fanned him with Chamaras whereas another lotus eyed one extended water to him.

पञ्चमं रत्नम्

One can notice a fine alliteration even in this chapter;

परिभ्रमन्त्यौ परितः पुरीं च तां पुरोऽवने स्तत्र शनैः पुरस्सरे।
परीतजाति प्रमुखप्रसूनकां वनीमपश्याव परीमलावनीम्॥[१]

The introduction of the character of Balaganapathi here speaks about the narrative genius of the poet;

ऽवं कंचित्समयं नीत्वा तत्र प्रतिनिवृत्ते बालिके मध्येमार्ग शुण्डादण्ड-मुत्सार्य तलझलत्पदकिङ्किणी निकूणानुगुणं भूरिकायोपरिचय च्छिरसा शिलोलूखल गर्तवर्यलावर्तमान शिलापिण्ड विड़म्बमानं लम्बमान महोदरमध्य कण्डूतिं करौ सुदीर्घं प्रसार्य कर्षन्तं परिभ्रमणरयान्निवर्त्य पश्चार्धमुपगतायाः परिस्पन्दि बन्धुर निलम्बबिम्बोपरि लम्बमानायाः, प्रालम्ब नायकमणेः प्रचण्डताण्डवं प्रदर्शयन्तं, नटन्तं वटुं बालं गणाध्यक्षमद्राक्षिष्ठाम्।[२]

The grandeur of the marriage of Hala is narrated next;

पुरकृतपुरोहितं पुरोगतपरीवार बन्धु मित्रसचिवबन्धुरं हैमवतीपशुपति समक्षम् पाशुपतस्वसाक्षिकं हालालीलावत्योः विधिविहितं मङ्गलस्वन-महितं विवाहं महावैभवमकारयत्॥[३]

In accompaniment of the priests, with the entire family in the front, along with relatives and friends in the presence of Shiva and Parvati along with the witnesses in accompaniment of the auspicious sounds Hala's marriage was celebrated in a grand scale.

---

1. *Ibid. p.* 87
2. *Ibid. p.* 82
3. *Ibid. p.* 97-98

षष्ठ रत्नम्

After Hala's reign his Son Mandulaka succeeded him. Here again, the alliteration catches our attention;

तस्य हालस्य राज्यान्ते अध्युवास तदासनम्
सुतो मन्दुलको नाम यज्ञस्तुन्दिल कान्तिधृत्।
जनकेन समो हि पालने जनकेनापि समश्च तत्वतः।
जनको यशसां च संपदां जनकल्यायित मूर्तिरैव सः॥[१]

After the end of the regime of Hala his son Mandulaka succeeded him who was on par with Janaka in the matters of looking after his subjects, in actuality, in his fame, money and he was the very embodiment of Janaka.

Next we have Gautamiputra Shatakarni's description who was a scholar,a poet, a poetic connoisseur, a born warrior and so on;

विद्वान्कविः पण्डितपक्षपाती महागुणो लोकनुतैकवीरः।
पवित्रवेदोक्तपदानुगस्स प्रभुर्बभौ गौतमिपुत्ररत्नम्॥[२]

The various preparations for the sacrifice which he undertook is graphically portrayed here;

तत्र धान्यम्महानगरे सवनशालायामाज्यहोम चिरपराचित वीतहोत्र नीलकेशशिखायित् हविर्गन्धजल धूमपटलपरिलक्षित नवाम्बुदागम् आयितगभीरनमोन्तराल बहुश्रुतिबहुश्रुत ऋत्विग्विततिवितत श्रुतिवाग्य प्लुति श्रीदिगुणीकृत सवनसमय समानीत समुन्नतकपिल धेनुजातां भाखाकीर्णकुसुम काताखरि कान्तारयक्षवाटिके वेदनिकरयाकरणतर्क मुखनिखिल विद्याविषयपरीक्षणादिगतविजय जनितमविघृतैकपाल दत्तबहुमानपुरस्सर महार्हमनम्बलौ चित्रवर्णीकृत सत्सदस्यसमा विभागा-भोग शोभाभासुरे यज्ञनारायण नामांकितोच्चावच रागरञ्जितगीति-

1. *Ibid. p.* 99
2. *Ibid. p.* 111

कारीतिकल्पित सभाजनप्रीतिरसैर्गायिकसार्वभौमैः कृत सङ्गीतापरस्वे सवनकर्मणि सम्पूर्णे दक्षिणा प्रददौ योग्याः प्रदक्षिणनमोविधाः। दक्षिणस्सर्वदानेषु विप्रेभ्यो गौतमीसुतः॥[1]

In that great city of Dhanyakataka in the sacrificial place the black smoke was emanating everywhere and thus making the whole atmosphere sacred, where in the different priests officiating the sacrifice were chanting different Vedas.There, one could perceive scholars in different branches of knowledge like Nyaya, Vya karana, etc and when the sacrifice came to an end with the music, the dakshina (money) was offered to the priests with pradakshina (by circumambulating them) and Gautamiputra Shatakarni considered the charities given to revered Brahmins as the greatest charities.

This Ratna comes to an end with a beautiful alliteration;

भवतीं भवती व्रतादिनीं
भवपत्नीं भवनाशिनीं शिवाम्
भवनीकृत् मुक्तमानसा
भविकश्रीकर वैभवां भजे॥[2]

सप्तम रत्नम्

Gautamiputra Shatakarni had a son by name Pulomaja. Just as the plants grow in spring so also that prince grew like the moon and women considered him to be the incarnation of Manmatha. He became a master of the various sastras with the grace of his teacher and also became an expert in warfare. He resembled Arjuna

1. *Ibid. p.* 110
2. *Ibid. p.* 111

in archery as well as protecting the needy, In the understanding of the vedas he was like the very Brihaspati and in charities he resembled Karna;

शम्भोस्तु श्रीमहाशरायां कुमार इव शक्तिमान्
तस्य राज्ञो महाराज्ञां पुलोमेति सुतोऽभवत्।
वसन्तमम्बाकर पल्लवान्तः प्रवर्धमानं च कुमारचन्द्रम्।
रतिं ददानं नितरां जनानामाहुश्च तं मन्मथमीवनार्यः॥
क्रमेण गुरूभिर्लब्ध सर्वशास्त्रविशारदः।
विशारमणपुत्रो ऽसावभून्न रणकोविदः॥
स धनुष्कलया महेन्द्रसूनुः
श्रितरक्षाकरणे महेन्द्रसूनुः
निगमेषु सरस्वतीकलत्रो
बहुदानेश्च सरस्वतीकलत्रः॥[1]

अष्टमं रत्नम्

The policy adopted by Shatakarni to encounter the enemies is graphically depicted here;

ऽकदैकान्ततया प्रकृतिमण्डलमानीय विकृतिहतिहति खण्डन समाचारे समुचित समालोचनमाचचार ऽकैकं हन्मो वयमुतैकदा सर्वविद्विषे हन्मः इति चिन्तयन्त ध्रधानैरेके नैव प्रबोधितस्तेषु। ऽकेनैकेन चेध्युद्धं मियिहयंत्यवशेषिणः। गकत्र शत्रुभिस्सर्वैः योद्धुं नश्यापि दुष्करम्

तस्माद्विभज्य प्रबलानि सेना
दलानि योग्यानि प्रथक्पृथज्ञः।
प्रेष्याणि सेनापतिमेकमेकं
नियुज्यतेषु द्विषतां परेद्युः॥
मूलबलैरधिक्बलै रधिकतले रात्मपदृणेऽश्माभिः
ख्यातव्यमरि निरोधनसाधन सम्पत्ति पत्तिनिकरैश्च।

1. *Ibid. p.* 123

इति सम्मन्त्रितं कार्यं मंत्रिणा तेन तद्धितम्।
सर्वानुमतमाकर्ण्य शातकर्णिर्महारथी॥[1]

Once Shatakarni having united his ministers discussed at length about the means of conquering the enemies. should we conquer the barriers one by one or shall we conquer all of them at the same time?

If we try to conquer the enemies one by one, then the rest of them will join together against us and it becomes difficult for us to face them when they are united.

Hence we should follow the policy of divide and rule.Hence, we should split all of them differently and send a separate army to encounter them. With the approval of all his ministers and important subjects he went ahead with his plans for execution. Here, the poet has described the rule of shatakarni as perfect Democracy.

नवम रत्नम्

The glory of this Shatakarni's son Gautamiputra Yajnasri Shatakarni is depicted in the last chapter;

कुमारवतंसो गौतमीपुत्र यज्ञश्रीशातकर्णी समधीत
सकलागम श्रुतिस्मृतिकलाकलापस्सन् यौवनं प्राप्य
स वंशकर्ता सकलारिजाते श्रियश्य हर्ता सुयशोविहर्ता
बुधोपकर्ता कुजप्रहर्ता महीं विधत्तेस्म भुजैकशक्त्या॥[2]

Gautamiputra Yajnasri Shatakarni having mastered Srutis, Smrtis, and having attained youth, that upholder of the family was confiscator of the wealth of his enemies

---

1. *Ibid. p.* 117
2. *Ibid. p.* 123

and was the helper of the good people and dispeller of the wicked and was ruling with his shoulder power. One can notice a nice alliteration even in this Stanza.

How the Shakas though afraid of Gautamiputra Yajanasri shatakarni were envious of him and instigated by others how they fought a bloody battle with him is picturesquely portrayed here;

शराभिवर्षेण शराभिवर्षः कृपाणघातैश्य कृपाणघाताः।
वज्रेण वज्रं तु विभिद्यते खल्यतीव तद्घोररणे नरस्ताः॥[१]

The arrows met the arrows, the swords were matched by swords, the Diamond was encountered with a diamond and ultimately the Shakas were defeated.

The following stanza has a fine Simili;

ऽवमत्र चलितं महोल्बर्ण तद्रणे कूणितसिञ्जनीगणे
उच्चलन् सपदि शतकर्णिराट्त शक मशकइत्यपातयत्॥[२]

In that fierce battle Shatakarni made the Shakas flee from the battle field just like the flies flee from a place.

The religious tolerance of Yajnasri Shatakarni is portrayed here;

सवर्धिष्णुः वैदिकमतसञ्जातोऽपि परमतसहिष्णुः स्वराज्ये सर्वतोभद्रं संपादयन्नपरसमन्नभद्रं बौद्धमतवामयायुर्वेद प्रचारकला समुपार्जनमाचार्य नागार्जुनं वैदिकमताचार्यैः समं निजसभायां सभाजयत् श्रीपर्वते तस्मै संघारामं निर्मापयित्वा तत्र तं संस्थाप्य तत रसुवान्बभूवलेखादिभिस्तत्क्षेम-मभिजानंस्त् बहु बहुमानितवान्र्बभूव॥[३]

That king although rooted in vedic tradition was tolerant towards the other religious and as a mark of

1. *Ibid. p.* 124
2. *Ibid. p.* 124-125
3. *Ibid. p.* 126

this he encouraged Buddhism, and Ayurveda and honoured the great Budhist logician Nagarjuna on par with the vedic scholars in his kingdom and built a budhist vihara called Sangharama for him in Sri parvata and looked after his well being on account of which he was highly regarded.

He was followed by his son Vijaya on whom the poet has construed a beautiful pun in the following stanza;

संग्रामलब्धविजयो वजयो विजयोपमः।
अजेयतेजा अकरोद्राज्यं षड्वर्षसम्मितम्॥[1]

He was victorious in the battlefield by name Vijaya and he had an unmatched radiance and made his enemy bereft of enemies for six years.

He was followed by Chandrasri who inturn was followed by Pulomani.

To conclude one can say that Rajaratnamala champu is endowed with many charming alankaras like उपमा, अनुप्रास, विराधाभास, उत्प्रेक्षा, युग्मक etc but the poet is at his best in अनुप्रास irrespective of whether it is a prose passage or poetry. The work serves as a very authentic historical record as it traces the rule of the important rulers belonging to a poet dynastry who ruled in Andhra for so long. The mastery of the poet over various Sastras like Vedanta, Vyakarana, Nyaya etc are also evident here.

1. *Ibid. p.*

2

SRISARVAJNENDRA CHAMPU GOVINDA BHATTA-1968

Sri Sarvajnendra Champu was written by Govinda Bhatta and published by Svarnavalli Maha Samsthan Sirsi in the year 1968 which traces the historical account of the Svarnavalli Mutt for which there is a reference in the first stanza itself;

ताः पान्तु सुवर्णविल्लि निलयां मां सर्वदाः दवताः[१]

The modesty of the poet is revealed in the third stanza;

कविता सविता नाहं किमपि न लेख्यं लिखेच्च मम हस्तः।
तदपि च विवुधैर्दयया परगुणपरमाणु तुष्टिरभिगाह्यम्॥[२]

The poet clearly states in the stanza four stanzas that his work is bereft of verbal jugglery and he has composed the work just to please the poetic connoisseurs;

मम किल कवितेयं शब्दबाहुल्यहीना तदपि बुधजनोऽयं तोषमे यादितीच्छा[३]

1. Sarvajnendra Champu-Govinda Bhatta, Svarnavalli Mahasa msthan, Sirsi, 1968, p. I.
2. *Ibid. p.* 1
3. *Ibid. p.* 1

The work is divided into स्तबक on the basis of Champu Bharatha and it has seven स्तबक or chapters. The work commences with a nice alliteraton;

अस्ति प्रशस्ता भुवि राजमाना नाकादिलोकानुपहासमाना।
प्रजाजनानां हितमादधाना अश्रीमत्सुधापूरित शोभमाना॥[१]

which has similarity with the following stanza of Bhoja's Champu Ramayana;

अस्ति प्रशस्ता जनलोचनानां आनन्दसन्धायिषु कोसलेषु।
आज्ञा समुत्सारित दानवानां राज्ञामयोध्येति पुरी रघूणाम्॥

The beautiful city was ruled by a king named Arasappa who was the very embodiment of valour and generosity, who was always treading on a wise path and vanquishing the wicked and who was respected by one and all;

यांशास्ति मन्यो ह्यरसत्पनामा त्वोदोर्यशौयर्दि गुणैकभूमा।
दुर्मार्गिहन्ता शुभमार्गगन्ता लोकैकपूज्यो भूवनैकराज्यः॥[२]

In the vicinity of that kingdom was established svarnavalli Mutt;

तेनाष्टसप्तत्यधिके चतुर्दशे सुशालिवाहे किलराक्षसेब्धे।
माधस्य कृष्णास्य चतुर्दशीतिथौ संस्थापितेऽयं सुवर्णविल्ली॥[३]

That mutt had the good fortune of having the two great ascetics by name Sarvajna and Gangadhara who had acquired immortal fame and who had sanctified the entire earth;

अलौकिकीं कीर्तिमुपार्जयन्तौ सच्छिष्यलोकानपि पावयन्तौ।
सर्वज्ञगङ्गाधर नामभाजौ यस्यां स्थितौ यतिराजमुख्यौ॥[४]

---

1. *Ibid. p.* 1
2. *Ibid. p.* 1
3. *Ibid. p.* 2
4. *Ibid. p.* 2

With this background, the poet says that now he tries to trace the background of the Mutt historically with the blessing of the great ascetics;

श्रीमन्मठसाध्य चरित्रमेतत्पुरातनीयं कथयन्ति तज्ज्ञाः।
वदामि सच्छिष्यगणैः सुबोद्धुं मनः प्रतुष्टै च गुरोः कृपायै॥[१]

When Shankaracharya was in Kashi once a Brahmin from Gokarna by name Viswapathi Bhatta's son got the सन्यासदीक्षा from Shankara. His disciple was Sarvajna Gangdhara peeth;

ततः प्रभृत्येव परंपराया सर्वज्ञगङ्गाधरपीठयुग्मम्।
संदृश्यतेनऽधापि पवित्रशब्दं तपः प्रभावैरतिपूज्यमानम्॥[२]

The place was inhabited by Havyaka Brahmins whose mother tongue was Kannada and they were devoted to religious duties;

तद्राज्यमध्ये परिपूर्णभाषा कर्नाटकी सर्वजनप्रचारे
ततः प्रभृत्यध्यतनेपि काले सा हव्यकानां किल मातृभाषा।
ते हव्यकाः श्रीयजनादिपूज्य षट्कर्ममार्गे निरता सदा वै
ताकर्मभेदेन विभिन्नशब्दैः समाह्वयन्त्येव जनाः समस्ताः॥[३]

The king who had no issues prayed to the goddess here and with her grace got a son and intern due to the gratitude he built a new Mutt on the banks of the river which had Shalmali trees.He also installed there the idols of Lakshmi Narasimha, Chandramouli, Vyasa, Ganesha, Shankara and sharada;

स राजवर्येण सुमान्यमानः स्वराज्य देवीमपि याचमानः।
स्वदेवतानुग्रहतः सुपुत्रं राज्ञेऽचिराद्वै प्रददौ यतीशः॥

1. *Ibid. p.* 2
2. *Ibid. p.* 3
3. *Ibid. p.* 4

तेनतितुष्टो ह्यरसप्पराजः श्रीशाल्मलीतीर समीपदेशे।
श्रीमन्मठं तत्र तु कारयित्वा लक्ष्मीनृसिंहस्य च चन्द्रमौलेः॥
व्यासे तथा शंकरपूज्यमूर्ति गणेशमूर्तिं च तदेव गेहे।
पृथक्सुगेहे वरशारदां तां क्षेत्राधिनाथं च बहिः प्रकोष्ठे॥[१]

From that day onwards the king gave equal attention towards the betterment of his kingdom as well as towards the development of the Mutt and he used to rule riteously with which his subjects were happy;

ऽकां दृष्टिं स्वराज्ये तदितरनयनं स्वणविल्यां निवेश्य।
धमत्मिा राज्यभारं व्यदधदतिचिरं स्वप्रजारंजकः सन्॥[२]

With the patronage of the king the name given to the Mutt Svarnavalli was really upto the name;

राजाश्रयात्पुण्य सुवणविल्ली यथार्यनाम्नी किल वै बभूव॥[३]

Here ends the प्रथम स्तबक which mainly concerns with the historical antiquity of the Mutt;

गोविन्दभदृविरचिते सर्वज्ञेन्द्रचम्पूग्रन्थे पूर्णकालिक
ऽतिहासिक परिचयो नाम प्रथमः स्तबकः।

द्वितीय स्तबक

Here the main subject matter is गङ्गाधरस्वामिना ब्रह्मीभूतस्थिति वर्णनम् Gangadhara Swamy who became the chief pontiff of that mutt was good at penance as well as in day to day activities;

यथा यतीन्द्रो व्यवहारधुर्यः तथा तपस्याप्यति धुर्यधुर्यः॥[४]

There is a fine alliteration in the following stanza;

---

1. *Ibid., p.* 4-5
2. *Ibid. p.* 5
3. *Ibid. p.* 6
4. *Ibid. p.* 6

यथा मृगेन्द्री मृगराजराजस्तथा यतीन्द्रो नटराज आसीत्

The popular proverb in Kannada is nicely brought out here;

वक्तुं हि सर्वं सुकरं न कर्तुम्[1]

Which reminds us of Karna's statement in the third act of Veni Samhara; वक्तुं सुकरमिदं, दुष्करं अध्यवसितुम् Again the popular proverb वृद्धानारी पतिव्रता is nicely brought out by the poet; वृद्धाश्च नार्यो हि पतिव्रता स्युः नो यौवनेता पतिमेकमाप्ता[2]

The difficulty of maintaining the सन्यासाश्राम is nicely brought out in the following stanza with an illustration of पराशर;

बाल्ये तु सन्यासपरिग्रहोऽयमन्यत कष्टेनहि साध्य ऽव।
पराशराध्याः किल पूज्यपादाः कौपीनबन्धे खलुतेप्यशक्ताः॥[3]

Probably the poet has the following stanza of वैराग्यशतक in mind while writing the above stanza;

विश्वमित्र पराशरप्रभृतयः वाताम्बु जीर्णाशनाः
तेपि स्त्रीमुखपंकजं सुललितं दृष्ट्वैव मोहं गताः ।
शाल्यन्नं सघृतं पयोदधियुतं ये भुंजते मानवाः
तेषां इन्द्रियनिग्रहो यदिभवेत् विंध्यःप्लवेत्सागरे ॥

Then Swamiji expressed his desire to handover the responsibilities of the Mutt in the hands of the people as the new pontiff was still young and he went to Varanasi for तीर्थयात्राः–

---

1. *Ibid. p.* 8
2. *Ibid. p.* 8
3. *Ibid. p.* 9

श्रीमान्गंगाधरेन्द्रो बुधजनसहितः पिङ्गले भाद्र कृष्णे
प्रायाद्वाराणसीं तां पुरमतिरूचिरां विश्वनाथाधिवासां
भागीरथ्यां त्रिकालं निरतिशयमुदा स्नानकर्मादि कुर्वन्
तत्रत्यैः पण्डितैस्तैः सममति मिलितो भाष्यचिन्तापरोऽभूत् ॥[१]

The following stanza

निजसुतविरहं कथमिव जनता सहत इतीयं ममचिन्ता,
मयिक्लि यतिपदगत वर्तिदुःख करज सुक्षिष्याद्विरहेण ।
ऽवं तयोर्विरह गद्गदकण्ठयोस्तत्संभाषणं श्रुतवता गुरुशिष्ययोर्हि ॥[२]

(How will the people bear the separation from their children if I being a pontiff has to suffer the separation of my junior?) makes us remember the underneath statement of शाकुन्तल :

यास्यत्यध्य शकुन्तलेति हृदयं संस्पृष्टमुत्कण्ठया
कण्ठः स्तंभितबाष्पवृत्तिकलुषः चिन्ताजड़ं दर्शनम् ।
वैक्लव्यं मम तावदीदृशमिदं स्नेहाद् अरण्यौकसः
पीड्यन्ते गृहिणः कथं नु तनया विश्लेषदुःखैर्नवैः ॥

(Kanva says if I have to suffer the separation from my foster daughter Shakuntala what about the condition of the parents when they send their daughter to their husband's place?). The new pontiff could not control his sorrow though being consoled by others when the Swamiji departed to the other world;

गुरोः परंधाम गतिं तु दृष्ट्वा तत्रत्यशिष्यैः परिसांत्वितोपि
अन्वर्थ सर्वज्ञपदेत्युषित्वा रुरोद दीर्घं प्रविमुक्तकण्ठः ॥[३]

---

1. *Ibid. p.* 9
2. *Ibid. p.* 10
3. *Ibid. p.* 11

तृतीयस्तबकः

भाष्यत्रयाभ्यसनं, श्रीचक्रपूजाप्रारंभ

In this स्तबक the विद्याभ्यास of the new pontiff is graphically depicted;

Ganesha Sastry of Gokarna who had acquired fame in teaching the students for eight years started imparting knowledge to the new pontiff;

गोकर्णवासी स गणेशशास्त्री शिष्यप्रबोधे किल लब्धकीर्तिः।
वर्षाष्टकं श्रीमठपण्डित सन्नध्यापयामास यतीश मुख्यान्॥[1]

Sarvajna Swamy studied Nyaya and Vedanta purva Bhaga under his tutelage;

सर्वज्ञयोगी गुरुष्वक्त्रपहमात्तर्क वेदान्तिक पूर्वभागान्।
अधीत्य विध्या कवितादि शक्तिं समार्जयामास सुब्रद्धिशक्त्या॥[2]

When the small Yati wanted to study further in Mysore under गुरुवालुकेश the mother was smitten with love and here Yati advices his mother where in the poet has introduced the very core of Advaita philosophy;

मिथ्यादृश्यमिदं च जगच्चनिखिलं भ्रात्यैवमूढ़ाजनाः
मे माता मम गेहिनी ममसुतो मद्गेहमित्यादिकान्।
अज्ञातावृतचेतनाः प्रतिदिनं मोहान्धकूपेस्थिताः
स्मारं स्मारमतीव तुष्टहृदया नो ब्रह्मते विन्दते॥
त्वं सर्वज्ञयतीशमूलजननी सर्वं विजानास्यहो
त्वद् बाह्येन्द्रिय दृश्यपुत्रममता दूरं परित्याज्यताम्।
ईदृक् ज्ञानयुतापि मोहजलधौ मूढ़ेवमग्नायदि
त्वत्तो न्यून वयस्कदूःखित जनान्कोवा समाधापयेत्॥[3]

---

1. *Ibid. p.* 11
2. *Ibid. p.* 12
3. *Ibid. p.* 13

The popular Subhashita धैर्यं सर्वत्र साधनम् is nicely brought out in the following stanza by the poet;

सर्वत्र धैर्यं खलु साधनं हि तेनैवकार्यं निखिलन्तुसाध्यं॥[1]

वालुकभारती

Valuka Bharathi was known as the lion among the Logicians, Vacaspati among the Vedantins and who was a scholar in the court of king Maharaja of Mysore and whose fame had spread far and wide;

यस्तर्कैमृगराड़िति प्रकथितो वेदान्तवाचस्पति
यो मैसूर महानृपस्य सदसोप्यास्थान विद्वानभूत्।
यत्कीर्तिश्च दिगन्त पण्डितवरैः काश्या च साकर्ण्यते
सोऽयं वालुकभारती पदगतं शास्त्री विरूपाक्षकः॥[2]

The statement माद्वीकमृद्वीक समानयोगः समागमोऽय गृरूशिष्य-योस्तु makes us remember the popular statement regarding the combination of prose and poetry viz champu;

स्वधेत सुधियः माध्वीक मृद्वीकयोः

The popular statement in Kannad is nicely brought out in the following stanza;

पुरातनीया किल गायिकेयं पापिष्ठमर्त्यो जलधिं प्रपन्नः।
निमज्जनेच्छुः प्रविशेध्यदातु सर्वत्रागाद्यः किलजानुदहनः॥[3]

चतुर्थः स्तबकः

In this chapter, the principal theme is returning

---

1. *Ibid. p.* 13
2. *Ibid. p.* 14
3. *Ibid. p.* 16

to his own Mutt from Koodli Mutt, Sri Chakraradhana and there is a beautiful Chamundi Stotra also.

Swamiji started the Sri chakra puja;

ऽवं तु दुःखान्नयनांबु मुंचन्नंबांब पाहीति सदावदताम् ।
श्रीचक्रपूजा निरतो नितान्तं निनायकालं यतिरग्रधैर्यः॥[१]

The daily routine of the Swamiji has been beautifully summed up in the following stanza;

श्री सर्वज्ञयतीश्वरः प्रतिदिनं यामे चतुर्थे निशि
स्नात्वा नित्यजपाह्निकादि सकलं निर्वर्त्य चक्रासनं ।
विध्याशंकरदेवतां गुरुवरै र्भ्यर्थ्यमानां सदा
संपूज्यातितरां प्रणम्य पुरतस्थित्वाच याचेवरम् ॥[२]

The Chamundi Stotra has been very effectively brought out next;

अये चामुण्डेशि प्रणत जगत्सर्वेष्टफलदे
त्वदीयो यं भक्तः स्थित इह पुरस्ताञ्जननिभो।
स्वदेशं गन्तासौ तवचरणयुग्मं परिहरत्
तथापि त्वं बालं नविसृजि दयाविष्टहृदया॥
प्रसन्नंते चित्रं यदि भवति लोकत्रयमपि
समृद्धं कर्तुं वै क्षणमपि नवंला प्रचलति।
अहं सर्वत्यागी यति पदगतो ह्यस्मिसुतरां
तथापित्वां याचे तवचरणसेवां त्वविरतम् ॥[३]

Then we have a beautiful contrast between death and poverty and it is said that poverty is worse than death;

दारिद्र्यं मरणं चेत्युभयं दुःखप्रदं लोके।
मरणादपि दारिद्रं चिरतरदुःखप्रदं ज्ञेयम्॥[४]

1. *Ibid. p.* 17
2. *Ibid. p.* 18
3. *Ibid. p.* 20
4. *Ibid. p.* 21

The same statement is echoed by charudatta in

मृच्छकटिक अल्पक्लेशं मरणं, दारिद्रमनन्तकं दुःखम्।

Then Swamiji through his penetic power eradicated poverty in that region;

ऽवं यतिः स्वीयतपःप्रभावा द्दारिद्रदुःखात्प्रविमोच्य सर्वान्।
उद्दारयामास सुवर्णवृष्ट्या यथापुरा ह्यनृपंयतीशः॥[1]

पञ्चम स्तबकः

The important events in this chapter are the visit of the Swamiji to Udipi, Dharmasthala, Gokarna and performance of candi Sacrifice.

UDUPI

The sacred place Udupi is endowed with eight mutts and there is also Sirur Mutt there;

क्षेत्रं सुरम्यं हुडुपीतिनाम्ना रराजतेह्यष्टमठैर्यतीशैः।
तेष्वेव शीरुकमठोपि कश्चित् लक्ष्मीन्द्रतीर्थो यतिरस्ति तत्र॥[2]

Then Sri Krishna Stotra has been effectively introduced here with a beautiful alliteration;

अनन्यभक्तियुक्त भक्तरक्षणे पणः कृतो
ह्ययं त्वदीय भक्तवर्ग्य पावनास्मि किं नुते।
उद्दवाध्यानेकभक्त वृन्दमुद्दरन्पुरा
निदर्शनं प्रदर्शितं स्वनीतिकोक्ति रक्षणे॥[3]

Then in the end Swamiji introduces himself to Sri Krishna that he has his Mutt Swarnavalli by name which is far off from here and requests the Lord to protect his people;

---

1. *Ibid. p.* 26
2. *Ibid. p.* 27
3. *Ibid. p.* 29

मठोयमस्ति दूरतः सुवर्णविल्लिनामकः
तत्रैवसीम्नि षोड्शास्ति शिष्यवर्ग ऽव मे।
मदीय यांचया त्वया तदेव शिष्यमण्डलं
प्रापाल्यतां निरन्तरं सुखं सदा प्रदीयताम्॥[1]

GOKARNA

The place Gokarna has been effectively introduced with the help of a following prose passage;

अथ कदाचिदखिल भूमण्डल मण्डनायमाने काश्यापित्रिस्थलेडपि श्रेष्ठतमे कोटितीर्थादि नानाविधा तीर्थसंकुले रावणेश्वर स्थापित श्रीमहाबलेश्वरादि बहुविध देवता सान्निध्य सहिते सूर्यचन्द्रयोः परिपूर्णास्त सन्दर्शक श्री महापश्चिमासमुद्र परिसरम्ये श्रीगोकर्णवासिभिः[2]

Once Swamiji thought of visiting the auspicious Gokarna which is more sanctified than Kashi on account of Kotiteertha and others where in we have the idol Mahabaleswara being installed by Ravana and where in we can witness the setting of the sun as well as the moon.

चण्डीयागवर्णनम्

Then we have a picturesque description of the चण्डीयाग with a beautiful alliteration;

किं वर्णयामोऽत्र सहस्त्रचण्डीयागस्य वैशिष्ट्यमतीवरम्यम्।
ऽकत्रवेदत्रयपाठघोषो ह्यन्यत्र ऋत्विगृहवनीय घोष।
स्वाहेति शब्दादपरत्र घोषो ह्यस्रयफट्कारूकहस्तघोषः
सहस्त्रशः प्राप्त जनास्यघोषो भेर्यादिवौन्द्रश्यक भांभघोषः
दीपोदराह्युद्भव यंत्रघोषो ह्यन्यत्रवद्घेः शंकरस्यघोषः
ऽक्त्र ढ़क्कादिवाध्यघोषो ह्यन्यत्र मौरीस्वनतः सुघोषः

1. *Ibid. p.* 29
2. *Ibid. p.* 30

आगतहव्यग्रहण प्रवृत्तसुरादि वैमानिकशब्दघोषः
हव्येन तुष्टाप्विल देवबृन्दैः सन्तोषतोवादित वाद्यघोषः।
सहस्त्रशः सप्तशतीय पाठैस्तदन्यतः खण्डित मारिकेरैः
तैस्तैः समुद्भूत विशेषज्ञशब्दैर्योत्येत शब्दास्यतु घोष घोषः।[1]

How to describe the beauty of the सहस्रचण्डी याग? At one particular place one could hear the chanting of the three Vedas and at some other place the voice of the priests offering various ingredients into the fire, at some other place the beating of the various instruments and the sound of the gods at the arrival of taking the sacrificial offerings and being pleased with that the sound generated by the gods and at still some other places the sound of the breaking of thousands of coconuts who were engaged in the chanting of सप्तशती

षष्ठ स्तबकः

In this chapter we have the vivid portrayal of काशीयात्रा, विश्वनाथदर्शनम्, गयायात्रा, गङ्गास्तुति, प्रयागगमनम् and others.

काशीयात्रा

सर्वज्ञयोगी शुभकृत्सुवत्सरे माघे सिते पूत चतुर्दशीतिथौ
शिष्येणयुक्तं गुरुवासरेवै यात्रादिनं निश्चिनुतेस्मकाश्या।
वाराणसी सर्वजनैकवंद्या तत्रापि हिन्दूजनपुण्यभूमिः
अतः समस्तामनुजा विशेभत्काशीं प्रयांत्येव सुभक्तियुक्ताः[2]

The great sage decided to go to Kashi on an auspicious day. Kashi is revered by everyone and it is a holy region of the Hindus and hence every one tries to visit Kashi atleast once in a life time.

---

1. *Ibid. p.* 33
2. *Ibid. p.* 35

विश्वनाथदर्शनम्

Here, a beautiful stanza has been introduced in the form of

विश्वनाथस्तुति:

विश्वनाथ विश्ववंद्य विश्वपापहारक
लब्धकाम ऽव सर्वथास्मि तेंध्रियुग्मकम्।
अहं तु धन्य ऽव सर्वथास्मि नोहि संशयो
यतोऽध्यतै हि दर्शनं तु भुक्तिमुक्तिदायकम्॥[१]

Lord Viswanatha is respectworthy in all the three worlds and he is the destroyer of the sins. Indeed, I am the most fortunate as I had your darshan today with which I became sanctified.

गयायात्रा

Swamiji also undertook a pilgrimage to Gaya from Kashi on an auspicious day;

माघेस्य कृष्णे दशमीतिथौ च वाराणसी तां हि गयां प्रयात:।[२]

The greatness of Ganga is vividly portrayed here;

नाममात्रपाठतोऽपि पाविता जनास्त्वया
दर्शनं समक्षतोऽद्य पूत ऽव सोस्म्यहम्।
स्नानपान पूजनादि यत्कृतं तवाम्भसि
तेन मुक्त ऽव सर्वथा न संशयो मम॥[३]

People will be sanctified by just uttering your name and I have been sanctified with your darshan and one who takes bath or offers prayers to you will be definettly liberated. There is a nice alliteration in the following stanza;

1. *Ibid. p.* 38
2. *Ibid. p.* 38
3. *Ibid. p.* 39

शैलराजशृङ्गतोवतारिणी विहारिणी
भवाब्धिमग्न सर्वलोकचारिणी सुचारिणी।
जह्नुकन्यके त्वदीय वारिबिन्दुपानतो
मृतोऽमृतो भवेद्धृवं पुनर्जनुर्भवेनवै॥[1]

प्रयाग प्रयाणम्

Then the great sage want to Prayag and took a holy dip at the meeting point of Ganga and Yamuna;

वाराणसीतो निरगात्प्रयागक्षेत्रं पवित्रं यतिराट् स्वशिष्यः।
स्नात्वाथ गङ्गायमुनासुसंगे कृत्वाऽथः पूजादिकमेव सर्वम्॥[2]

सप्तम स्तबकः

In this last स्तबक we have the accounts of Ayodhya Haridwar, Delhi and the installation of a new Sharada shrine.

अयोध्या

The beauty of Ayodhya is beautifully depicted here;

अयोध्यापुरं सुन्दरैमन्दिरैर्वा सुशोभायमानं यशोभासमानम्।
प्रविश्याथ रामं सुसीतां च पूतां तथा लक्ष्मणादीश्च दृष्ट्वासुगेहे॥[3]

Ayodhya is beautiful with the temple of Rama and swamiji also perceived Sita and Lakshmana idols there.

हरिद्वार ऋषिकेष

The sanctity of Haridwar and Rishikesh as perceived by Swamiji is nicely delineated here;

---

1. *Ibid. p.* 40
2. *Ibid. p.* 43
3. *Ibid. p.* 43

यतिर्हरिद्वारसमाश्रितं तस्साप्तर्षि मुख्याश्रममण्डलं हि
पृथक् पृथक्वीथय विशेषतुष्टश्यूतादिवृक्षैः सुमनोहरं च।
ततो ययौ क्षेत्रमतीव पूतं नाग्ना हृषीकेशमितिप्रसिद्धं
तत्रत्य रामादि सुमूर्तिवृन्दं महामुनीनां च सुमन्दिराणि॥[१]

The Swamiji saw the hermitage of the seven sages differently and was immensely happy regarding the whereabouts of the people which abounded within the mango trees from there he proceeded to Rishikesh and saw the temples pertaining to different gods.

At a distance Swamiji perceived Himalayas which Kalidasa has so vividly perceived in his Kumara Sambhavam;

अस्त्युत्तरस्यामिति कालिदासो यं वर्णयामास हिमालयं तम्।
तादृक्महामूर्ति सुवर्णितस्य तस्यैव शक्नोति हि वर्णने कः॥[२]

दिल्ली

Then Swamiji went to Delhi which was known as Hastinavathi in history;

ईदृक्महाक्षेत्रमिदं विमुच्य दिल्लीपुरं तच्च जगाम योगी।
यदेवपूर्वं किल हस्तिनाख्यं वदन्ति सर्वेत्वितिहासतज्ञाः॥[३]

There Swamiji perceived Kutub Minar, Red Fort and president Radhakrishnan;

कुतूपमीनाराव्य मस्त्यतीव सुन्दरं, परं ददर्श रक्तसच्छिलानि बद्धदुर्गमुत्रमम्।
राष्ट्राध्यक्षं मुदानाम्ना राधाकृष्णं ददर्श सः॥[४]

1. *Ibid. p.* 44
2. *Ibid. p.* 45
3. *Ibid. p.* 45
4. *Ibid. p.* 46

INSTALLATION OF THE NEW SHARADA SHRINE

Swamiji thought of installing a new Sharda Shrine as the earlier one had become slightly mutilated;

ऽवं जनानां मुखतो विदित्वा मूर्ति मठस्यामपि शारदायाः।
जीर्णां विलोक्यातितरां च खिन्नो निर्मापिनेच्छुः किल तां च नूत्नाम्॥[1]

After this, we have ग्रन्थकर्तु परिचय with which we come to know that the author has compsed this work with the grace of the Swamiji Sarvajna Yati;

सर्वज्ञयोगीन्द्र कृपाकटाक्षाऽग्रन्थं च चम्पूमयमेव पूज्ये।
विरच्य छात्रालय शिष्यवृन्द दृगंगणे स्थापयति प्रमोदात्॥[2]

The love of the poet towards the popularity of Sanskrit Language is clear with the following stanza wherein we have a charming alliteration;

वरीवर्तुर्गीर्वाण वाणीजगत्यां नरीनर्तुसैवाद्य जिह्वांगणेमे।
चरीचर्तुसर्वोपि यत्नं तदर्थं सरीसर्तु दूरं विलंबश्चजाड्यम् ॥[3]

To conclude, one may say that this Champu is unique in the sense that it is a historical record, as well as a travelogue. It historically traces the background and the happenings of the Svarnavalli Mutt as well as gives a pen picture of the important pilgrim centes of India. some of the idiomatic expressions of Kannada Language have been incorporated here. The work also can serve the purpose of a Stotra Kavya as some of the Stotras introduced here are highly devotional.

The style of the poet is simple, lucid and straightforward and in the end he has given his family background also under the section ग्रन्थकर्तृ परिचय।

---

1. *Ibid. p.* 48
2. *Ibid. p.* 53
3. *Ibid. p.* 53

3

SRI SHARANNAVARATRA CHAMPU-K.KRISHNA JOIS-1976

Sri Sharannavaratra Champu is a champu work composed by Pandita Pravara K.Krishna Jois depiciting the annual festivities held in Sringeri during the auspicious Navaratri Celebrations, and Published by Sharada Gourava Granthamala in the year 1976. The work consists of six chapters and each chapter has been given a name such as वराहपर्वतवर्णनम्, श्रीमठवर्णनम्, श्रीशारदाम्बा अभिषेकवर्णनम्, श्रीशरन्नवरात्रोत्सवारम्भवर्णनम्, द्वितीयादि चतुर्थ्यन्तोत्सववर्णनम् and पञ्चम्याद्येकादश्यन्तोत्सववर्णनम्।

An attempt is made in the following pages to evaluate the work as a sample survey.

The poet commences the work in the form of नमस्कारात्मकमङ्गल wherein he has offered his salutations to Sri Shankaracharya, chandrasekhara Bharathi Swamiji and Abhinava Vidyatirthaa Swamaji's:—

शङ्खरूपेण मच्चित्तं पङ्क्तीकृतमभूद्यथा।
किङ्करी यस्य सा माया शंकराचार्यमाश्राये।

राजाधिराज मुकटाग्र मणिप्रदीपैः
नीराजितेम्नगाश्रय यमार्चिते च।
श्री चन्द्रशेखर जगदगुरुपादपद्म
युग्मे प्रणामकुसुमाञ्जलिमर्पयामि॥
विद्यानर्ध्ये तपोनिधेगुरुवराल्लब्धोपदेशार्जित्
श्रीविधा जननी प्रसादवितत श्रीकीर्तिविद्याञ्चितान्।
चन्द्रभानन सुन्दरान् मृदुवचः पीयूषमुग्धाखिलान्
विद्यातीर्थ गुरुन् नवान् वयमिमान् वन्दामहे सादरम्॥[१]

वराहपर्वतवर्णनम् and शृङ्गगिरिक्षेत्रवर्णनम् are the two principle descriptions in the first chapter.

वराहपर्वतवर्णनम्

The scenic beauty of the वराहपर्वत is realistically portrayed here;

विराजने किल निखिलकलशिखरश्रेणि भूषणायमानस्य सभूघरस्य प्रत्यन्नपर्वतपंक्तिषु प्रत्यग्दिगङ्गनाविहार भूमिरिव विशीभमानः, पाताल तल निलीन भूमि समुद्धरणाय अवतीर्णेन आदिवराहर-वामिना आध्युषितमात्र पवित्रीकृतात्मा सुप्रथिदिभिधानः, वनराजिविराजमान पुन्नाग, नाग, चम्पक, चूत पनसादि तरुवराच्छादित प्रान्तप्रदेशः, अन्तरान्तराचित फलभरावनम्र रम्भातरू चर्यमाण शिशिरोपचार पुरस्कृताभिः फलभरमुग्न कन्धराभिरपि साहङ्काराभिरेव गगनोन्नमित कन्धराभिः पूगवृक्षराजिभिः समन्तात् सेव्यमानः, झंकार नाद परिपूरित वनान्त विराजमानाम्बरतल स्पर्शिशाखावलम्बमानालपतर जीमूत डाङ्कम्र मधुकर मधुकोशान्धकारित वनान्तः, प्राकृतिक रामणीयक दूरीकृत निखिल जनपद वनश्रेणिभिः नैकविधाग्रहाराश्रम देवागारान्तरित पुण्यक्षेत्र पावनीभ्यां तुङ्ग भद्राधेयाभ्यां तरङ्गिणीभ्यां परिशोभमानः वराहपर्वतो नाम पर्वतराजः॥[२]

1. Sri Sharannavaratra Champu-K.Krishna jois. Sharada Gourav Granthamala, Pune, 1976. p.I.
2. *Ibid.* p. 2

There is a king among the mountains named Varaha which is like the ornament to the Sahya mountain, which is like the path where the heavenly damsels move about, which has been made sanctified on account of the dwelling of Adi Varahaswamy who took his incarnation to uphold the earth which had merged in the nether worlds, which is abounding in various trees like Champaka, Asoka, Punnaga, Naga, Choota, Panasa, which have borne fruit on account of which the branches have bent down and thus catches the attention of everyone, because of the fragrance of various flowers the bees have appeared with two sacred rivers like Tunga and Bhadra on whose banks many hermitages and temples have come up.

In the above description one can find a beautiful Alliteration.

शृङ्गगिरिक्षेत्रवर्णनम्

Next we have a realistic description of Sringeri the holy pilgrimage;

ततः प्रदक्षिणं पश्चिमतः पूर्वदिशापिमुखं प्रवहन्ती तुङ्गातरङ्गिणी, स्नानपानाभ्यां यत्र महापातकिनमपि देवलोक अधिरोपयन्ती गङ्गायाः अनुकरोति। तटम् उपस्थितेष्वपि धीवरेषु निजकुटुम्बिनीभिः शिशुमिद्म हिरन्ति मस्त्य मकरादीनी वियादांसि जननीव अपत्यानि निर्विहाङ्गानि परिपालयन्ती आपगान्तराणि अपि अवधीरयन्ति चेयं तुङ्गापगां यस्य च नामश्रवणमात्रेण अवनीतलवासिनः समेऽपि निजशरांसि फलभरावनमतः तरवः इव आनामयन्ति, यरय च साधोरिव दर्शनम् सुदूरम् अध्युषित जनपदाः अपि जनाः निजजन्म चातुधि दपि सार्थयितुम् उत्सहन्ते यस्य च महात्मनः इव महिमभूम्नः श्रुतिपथावतरणमात्रेण आजन्मनिवास भूमिमपि क्षेत्रोत्तममपि मनसैव अवधीरयन्ति, यस्मिन् महामहिमशालिनि सज्जने इव सकृदपि दृष्टे

सर्वस्वमपि धनकनकादि सन्यस्य आर्जवं देहयात्रां घनकनकादि सन्यस्य आजीवं देहयात्रां परमान्मचिन्लया अतिवाहयितुं कामयन्ते। यत्र च भगवत्पादा अपि मठस्थापनाय स्थानमन्विष्यतः तुङ्गक निक्षा विस्तृत फणातपत्रेण भुजङ्गमेन निवार्यमाणातप संतापम्, आसन्न प्रसवां भेकीम् ΓΙकां निर्वर्ण्य साद्भुतं विनिणयिांचक्रुः-अयमेव प्रशस्तः प्रशान्तश्च समुद्देशः मठस्थापनाय इति। यत्र च समग्र भूमण्डल विस्तृतकीर्तिः श्रीमज्जगदि्गुरु वारालंकृतः श्रीदक्षिणाम्नाय पीठ विशोभमानो मठो विराजतेतमाम्। यच्च चतसृष्वपि दिशासू श्रीदुर्गा कालिकाभ्यां, कालभैरव हनूमद्भ्यां श्रीमदाचार्यपवित्रहस्त प्रतिष्ठिताभ्यां क्षामड़ामराद्युपद्रवेभ्यः सुरक्षितम्, यदत्र श्रीमच्छंकर भगवत्पादामृत हस्त प्रतिष्ठापित श्रीचक्रविद्योतमानया विद्याधिदेवतया, कामितार्थपूरणैक करुणापाङ्गवीक्षणया श्रीशारदाम्बया विद्योतते तदिदं श्रीश्टङ्गगिरि क्षेत्रं निखिल भारतजनयात्रा स्थानं भुवि विजयतेतराम्।[१]

Here we have the flowing of the river Tunga from West to the East by taking bath there or by sipping whose water one's sins will wash away which is in keeping with the adage. तुङ्गापानम् On the banks of Tunga we can notice the wandering fisherman and this Tunga has also given shelter to many fishes and crocodiles. By listening to that very name people bend their head in adoration like the trees which bends on account of the weight of the fruits. People throng to this place with great reverence as though to have the Darshan of a Great man. The atmosphere here is so soothing to the visitors that they feel like settling down here. Even Shankaracharya also in search of a fitting place to establish the Mutt came to this spot and decided that this is the ideal place to establish mutt as it is abounding in peace and tranquility, and hence we have the famous Mutt here in the South established by

1. *Ibid.* p. 3-4

Shankara. In all the four directions of which we have Sri Duga, Kalika, Kalabhairava and Hanuman which Shankara himself established through his pious hands which has been protected even to this day against calamities. Shankara also installed Srichakra and the revered Sharada who can fulfill the desire of her devotees with her gentle smile. Thus, this Sringeri is the pilgrim centre of the entire country.

श्रीमठवर्णनम्

This chapter narrates the curiosity of the people to witness the Navaratri festival, dress and anointment of the people, people's reaction having the Darshan of Swamiji, topography of the Mutt, the greatness of Tunga and so on.

We have a beautiful मालोपमालंकार in the following description of the people who were so curious to see the Navaratri festival;

सर्वतो दिग्म्यो विदिग्श्य श्रीशारदा शरन्नवरात्र महोत्सव दिदृक्षवः पलितशिरसोऽपि, जराहताङ्गभङ्गाः अपि, भुग्नावलग्नाः अपि, देवीदर्शने समुच्छलित कौतुकेन प्रत्यायात तरुणावस्थाः प्रायो जनाः। कटी तटिषु वाम भुजलता वेष्टितैः आताम्रकलशैरिव शिशुभिः कदाचन गौरांग्यो युवतयः, कराग्रावलम्बित वर्णरञ्जितायास पेटिकाः कक्षावलम्बित सितकम्बले मयाल्पतर भूताश्च, केचन श्रीत्रिय शिरोमणयः, आतप विसरा सहिष्णवः। उक्ष्णीशवेष्टित मूर्धानश्च खल्वाटाः। चक्षुष्मत् कटप्रसारित दण्डाग्रदर्शित मार्गाश्च अन्धाः, करतालमात्र बोधितपथा बधिराः उग्रतालेमात्र चेष्टा, पाणिचेषमात्रावगत सरणयो मूकाश्च, अपमूकाश्च दीनाः 'अक्ञ्चिनाः, पङ्गवः, कुणयः तीर्थयात्रयाऽपि निज जन्म हीनता निदान पाप निचय दूरीहरणोत्सवः शकटविशेषेभ्यःप्रतिपदम् अवतरन्ति हि असंख्यात संख्याकाः जनपदान्तरवासिनः प्रतिवत्सरं श्टङ्गगिरौ॥[1]

1. *Ibid.* p. 5

People had ascended there from different directions who were curious to witness Sharada Sharannavaratri festival. Though some of them had grown old with grey hair, whose body had become shrunk had appeared to be in their youth because of their curiosity in having the Darshan of Devi, some women had come there by carrying their children, there were some priests who had assembled there with their accessories, some bald headed people had come there who had covered their head with the woolen caps, there were blind, dumb, lame and others in large numbers who assemble every year to witness festivity.

DRESS AND ANOINTMENTS OF THE PEOPLE GATHERED

Next, we have a realistic portrayal of the dress and anointments of the people who had assembled there;

प्रान्तग्रामीणाः पुमांसो विविध वर्णोष्णीष पट्टालंकतोत्तमाङ्ग परिहित पीताम्बराः, स्त्रियश्च अर्धचन्द्राकृति कुंकुम तिलकाञ्चित निटिलाः, हरिद्रा चूर्णानुरञ्जित पादकपोलाः, मणिमय ताटङ्क भासुरेन्द्रवदनाः, कनकवलय पीतिमोज्वल कन्क्मलाः कराग्रानुनीयमान बालकबालिकाश्च युवतयः साक्षात् अम्बिका इव अवभासमानाः परापतन्तिच, यान्ऽगतान् अवलोकयतां समुझृंभते हृदये अपरिमितानन्द प्रवाहः, हृष्यन्ति च रोमाणि, विकसन्ति च वदनानि भक्तिश्च लोकमातरीव अङ्कुर पल्लव पलाश कुसुमकचावस्थाभिः तेनेव अभिवर्धते।[१]

The men who had come from different places had covered their face with woolen clothes of different colours, some of them were wearing pitambaras, the women had anointed their face with the Kumkum in the form of the crescent moon and whose face and

1. *Ibid.* p. 5

legs were covered up with saffron, some of the women were appearing like the incarnations of the goddess Ambika by perceiving whom the heart will be filled with joy, there will be horripulation all round, faces will blossom forth and the devotion will naturally set in.

Next we have the reaction of the people on witnessing Swamiji;

श्री चन्द्रशेखर जगद्गुरु पादपदमच्छायोपसेवि वरनूत्न जगद्गुरुणाम्।
सन्दर्शन त्वरूणदर्शनमग्रिमं च यात्रार्थिनोऽखिल जनस्य विबोधनाय॥
श्रीचन्द्रशेखरजगद्गुरु दिव्य वक्त्र सन्दर्शनं सुकृतिमात्रजनैः सुलभ्यम्।
यत्पावनं सकलपापविशोधनेन प्रातः प्रभाकरमण्डल दर्शनं नः।
अधैव जन्म सफलं फलितं च पुष्यं जन्मान्तरार्जित महार्जिधमात्मनो॥
अधैव जीवितमिदं परिपूतमन्यत् सर्वं कुलं च गुरुसन्निघि मागतस्य।
क्षेत्रे पवित्रे श्रुतिघोषतश्च, नेत्रे पवित्रे जननीविलोकात्।
जिह्वा पवित्रा वरतीर्थ पानात्ः घ्राणं पवित्रं जननी प्रसादात्।
शीर्षं प्रपूतं कुसुमप्रसादैः फलं च देव्याः वरकुङ्कमेन॥
अन्तः प्रपूतं किल चन्द्रमौलेः श्रीसद्गुरुणाच पदाब्जतीर्थैः॥
क्षेत्रस्य यात्रा रणेन पादौ पूजाप्रणामंश्च करौ प्रपूतौ।
वाक् चाम्बिकानाभसहस्र जायैः मनश्च देवी परिचिन्तनेन॥
अङ्गनिदण्डानतिमिश्च देहो देव्या यथाशक्ति निषेवणेन।
पुत्राश्च मित्राण्यथ बान्धवाः मे सर्वे कृत्यर्था स्म इहागमेन॥[1]

Having the sight of the newly consecrated pontiff (Abhinava Vidyateertha) before the Darshan of Chandrsekhara Bharathi Swamiji was like the Darshan of the Rays of the sun before the rising of the sun.

To Perceive the Effulgent face of Chandrasekhara Bharathi Swamiji was possible only on account of the merits being amassed in the previous births. His Darshan

1. *Ibid.* p. 6

would dispel all our sins just as with the emergence of sun, the darkness Dispels.

People thought that today their life had been gratified on account of the merits accumulated of the previous births. Having come to the sacred place of Swamiji, our entire Family has been purified.

By listening to the chanting of the Vedas the ears have been blessed, the eyes have been blessed with the Darshan of the Goddess, the tongue has been purified on account of the sipping of the sacred waters and by smelling the Prasada of the goddess, the nose has been gratified.

The head has been sanctified on wearing the flowers of the goddess, the face has been sanctified on account of applying the Kumkum of the goddess, the legs have been gratified on account of walking in the holy place and the hand has been blessed on account of doing Pooja and doing Namaskarams With folded hands. The speech has been purified on account of chanting the name of the goddess repeatedly, the mind has been purified with the thought of the goddess.

The various limbs have been blessed on account of sitting in proximity to goddess and all my sons, friends and relatives have been gratified by witnessing this place.

TOPOGRAPHY OF THE MUTT

अथ प्रविष्टमात्राः दक्षे पार्श्वे श्रीगुरुराजैः प्रतिहायनमपि चतुर्षुमासेषु कृत चातुर्मास्य संकल्पैः आराधमानस्य श्रीचन्द्रमौलीश्वरस्य भव्यं प्रासादं। वामे च पार्श्वे प्रतिवत्सरमपि पौरजन चर्यमाण भजनमन्दिरं, श्रीराम पञ्चायतन मूर्ति विलसितं, तया तत्रैव श्रीमठरक्षादीक्षितस्य प्रौढ़प्रतापशालिनः ब्रह्मदेवस्य भवनम्, अग्रतश्च

श्रीजगद्गुरु महासंस्थानीय धर्मकार्य निर्वहण व्यवहार स्थानं मुखमण्डपं च श्रीमठस्य, अग्रे च तपः प्रभावोज्वलीकृत धर्म पताकायमान सुवर्ण कलश चतुष्टय मध्य भास्वरतप्त चामीकर शिखर भूषितोन्तमाङ्गं त्रयस्त्रिंशत्कोटि देवता परिमण्डतं, मत्स्यादि दशावतार पुरुषैः परिपूजितम्, द्वादशाभिः मेषादि राश्यधिपत्यधितिष्ठतैः तत्तन्मान सोद्यदिनकर प्रसरमात्रेण चित्रवर्णानुरञ्जितैरिव भास्वद्भिः, वीर पुरुषाधिष्ठित मृगराजस्तम्भैः अन्तरेव उद्रधृत, जक्कणाभिधानेन अपर विश्वकर्मणा विनिर्मितम्, पश्चात् च त्रिमूर्त्यधिष्ठितैः त्रिभिः द्वारैः पुरश्च त्रिभिरिति षड्भिरङ्गैः इव दर्शनैः इव च पुरस्कृतम्, दुर्गा गणपति परिसेव्यमानस्य लम्बिकायोगनिष्ठस्य जगदीश सायुज्य साम्राज्य पीछाश्रिषिक्तस्य श्री विद्यातीर्थमुनि पदाभिगीतस्य, श्रीविद्या-शंकरगुरोः देवालयं च देवरथः इव विराजन्तं साचर्यं निभालय प्रलम्बितावयवाः! तदुपक्ण्ठेऽव आञ्जनेय गरुड़ोपसेव्यमान जनार्दन देवागारं, पश्चिमदिशि कनक्शिखर भासुरं श्री शारदाम्बा प्रासादम्, अपर भगवान् पादोपगीयमान श्रीसच्चिनदानन्द शिवाभिनव नृसिंहभारती स्वामिनाम् अमृतमय करकमलाभ्यां प्रतिष्ठापितां श्रीसद्विद्यासञ्जीविनी महापाठशालां, छात्रगणाधीयमान वेदधोषनिषेव्यमाण भगवात्पादमन्दिरं च दक्षिणाम्नाय कतिपयानां आचार्यवराणां विदेहकैवल्य मन्दिराणि च्छात्रवसित अन्नसत्रं च दूरादेव पश्यन्तः तुङ्गातरङ्गिण्याः परे तीरे च अूदूरतः जाम्बू नद श्टङ्गशेखर श्री शिवाभिनव नृसिंह भारतीनां भूमण्डलाचायर्णिां तपश्चक्रवर्ती पदसमारोहणेन स्वचरण नलिने परिपालितेन दिगन्तसंयमिनां विदेहकैवल्य साम्राज्याधिगत नित्यनिरा-निशयानन्द मन्दानुभूतिना मन्दिरेण, तदन्तिक विराजमानेन श्री चन्द्रमौलीश्वर सान्निध्य पवित्रीकृतेन श्रीसच्चिदानन्द विलासाभिधेयेन आश्रमं च भूपतिं श्री नृसिंहवनं नाम तपोवनं विलोकयन्तः ऽव हर्षोद्भूत रेामहर्षणाः सोपानमार्गेण अच्छाछाजलां तुङ्गातरङ्गिणीम् अवतीर्य मणिमय भूमिमिव तामन्ययत्॥[1]

1. *Ibid.* p. 6-7

As soon as we enter to the South we have Lord Chandramouliswara wherein the Swamijis commence their chaturmasya, To the left, we have the idol of Rama panchayatana and the Bhajan Mandir of the people, we also have Brahmadeva and then we have the Mukha Mandapa of the Mutt, then thirty three thousand deities, the incarnations of Visnnu, the chiefs of the constellations being erected by Jakana the second creator, then we have Sri Vidya Shankara Temple and nearer to that we have Janardhana temple and towards the west we have goddess sharadamba and also the Sadvidya Sanjivini Patashala being started by Sacchidananda Shivabhinava Nṛsimhabharathi Swamiji who was considered as the incarnation of shankara himself, then we have the Bhagavadpada Mandira wherein one can perceive the vedic chanting of the students. We also have the temples of Sureswara and others. We have in the vicinity Sri Narasimhavana which on being gazed creates a sense of horripulation.

GREATNESS OF TUNGA

The greatness of Tunga is well portrayed here;

स्नानं यद्बहिरन्तरं मलापकर्षत्यशेषं नृणाम् दानं यद्
द्विगुणीकरोति सफलं यत्रैव किंचित्कृतम्
पानं यन्मधुरीकरोति रसनां क्षाराम्बुपानाज्जड़ाम् तानिमानि
सुदुर्लभानि सुकृतैस्तुङ्गाऽध नोऽलक्ष्यत॥[1]

The bath here will cleanse us inwardly as will as outwardly. If one gives charities there, it will have double the fruit.If we sip the water there, it sweetens our tougue and thus river Tunga is a multipurpose river. How

1. *Ibid.* p. 8

men and women appear at the time of taking bath is pen pictured here;

तत्र च भवान्तरसंचित महापातकोपपातकमय मलापकर्षणाय चीर्णमज्जन संकल्पाः तटिनीतीर्थ निःशशंकं निमज्जन्तः उन्मज्जन्तश्च केचन, कतिपये चान्ये आनदीम्पश्याः शीतभीताः इव ताम्रघटया नदीजलम् आपायापाय स्वोत्तमाङ्गे निषिञ्चन्तः, अपरे च महामतस्य शीता तटे ऽव तिष्ठन्तः तोयम् उद्धृन्योघृत्य स्वाङ्गेषु सेचयन्तः, कथमपि पूर्णस्नानाः धृत धौतवाससः कृत भस्मत्रिपुण्डाः, स्त्रियश्च परिहित महाम्बरा कुंकुमाच्चिततिलकाः हरिद्राचूर्णविलेपित कपोले कर चरणाः, प्राचीनाचारान् अनुसरन्त्यः, प्ररन्ध्रः ताम्र राजत कास्यानाम अन्यतमेन कलशेन आपः आदाय तीरे विराजन् वृषभेन आसेव्यमान शिविलिङ्ग ताभिरिद्भिः अभिषिचन्त्यः, तथा बोधिद्रुममभितः प्रतिष्ठापितानां नागेन्द्राणां फणामण्डलेषु हालाहलचोपशमनाय इव जलम् उस्रावयंन्यः। बोधिद्रुम नामप्रतिमादूत प्रदक्षिणीकृत्य मूलतो ब्रह्मरूपायेति स्तुवंत्यो नमंत्यश्च, चिन्तित पुत्रादि फलानि प्रार्थयन्त, नमंत्यश्च, प्रार्थयन्तश्च, श्री शारदाम्बापरिलक्षणकौतुकिन्यः चतुःषष्ठिमित योगिनी गणाः इव भासमानाः पतिक्रियतेजस्तिरस्कृत परप्ररूषदृष्टयः पुरुषाश्च भास्कराय अर्चिताध्याः। कृष्णाजिनेषु कुश वस्त्रायासनेषु वा बद्य पद्मासनाः, रुद्राक्षमालिमभिः तुलसीमालाभिः वा जपन्तः, नास्तिकानामपि वैदिकेषु कर्मसु श्रद्धाभक्तिः आदधतः, परिसमापित विहितनित्यकर्मणः शारदाम्बा मुखपङ्कजस्य दर्शन सुखमनुभवतः इत्थं संलपतिस्म–

पार्श्वे दक्षिणातो विभाति च गुरोव्यख्यिानसिंहासनम्
पश्चात्पश्चिमतोऽपरं गणपतेः सन्मन्दिरं मन्दिरम्।
भक्त्या यत्र विशेषतः समुदिताः विद्यार्थिना नित्यशः
कुर्वंत्यर्चन मात्मनीनमनघं पक्षे प्रदोशेषु च॥[1]

There as though to dispel all their sins people

1. *Ibid.* p. 8-9

were taking bath. Some of them who had never come across a river in their life were afraid of cold and hence were pouring in water on their heads with the help of a copper vessel and still some others were standing on the banks with the fear of the presence of large fish approaching them and from there itself they were pouring in water from a distance. After taking bath they were smearing Tripundra to their foreheads and the women were annointing themselves with Kumkum and had smeared saffron to their cheeks and legs who were following the tradition and they were bringing in water and doing Pooja to shivalingas with either copper or silver or bronze vessels and they were also circumambulating the Bodhi tree and Nagas, some of them were chanting Mulato Brahmarupaya and some others were praying for the birth of the sons and they appeared as the sixty four yogins who were all chaste. Men used to offer Arghya to Sun, some wearing the deer skin and had seated in padmasana. They were doing japa with the help of the rosary beads or the garland of Tulasi or Sphatika. This act of theirs used to make even heterodox people orthodox. Having completed their rites they circumambulated the gods and then appeared as though they were going to heaven alive. They were experiencing the pleasure of perceiving the radiant face of the goddess.

To the South of the Goddess we have the sacred seat of the saints. Then we have the temple of Ganapathi wherein thousands of students offer their worship everyday in the morning and the evening.

शारदाम्बा अभिषेकवर्णनम्

The Abhisheka to Devi is graphically portrayed here;

दुग्धाभिषेककरणात् किल सर्वतोऽपि
दुग्धं दुहन्ति बहुलं भुवि धेनवोऽद्धा।
सन्दर्शनादपि नरोऽस्य च शारदेन्द्र
संकाशमेव सुपिषन्ति पयोऽमृतायम्॥

आज्येन स्नपनं यदम्ब! परया भक्त्या कृतं च त्वयि
त्वेतद्दर्शनिभागिनोऽपि मनुजाः आयुः शतं यान्तिहि।
आज्यं येन च भुज्यतेऽधिकतो भोज्यं च दीर्घायुषम्
तेनैवेति वृथा वदन्ति हि नराः नो दृष्टदेवीमुखाः॥

देवित्वांमधुना नितान्तमधुरेणापादशीर्षं परम्
संस्नाप्यापि न तेम्ब मूर्तिमतुला माधुर्यमित्रोजयत्।
किं त्वस्यानघ दर्शनेन हृदये वाङ्मानसागोचरम्
माधुर्यं परमं निरन्तरमहो धीराः स्वदन्ते ध्रुवम्॥[1]

By doing Abhisheka through curds, oh goddess, I am offering my Pooja to you.

Oh mother, now I am offering my respects to you in the form of offering ghee to you with utmost devotion. With your Darshan People can live upto hundred years. Those who eat ghee more, their longevity will increase. Here the poet seems to have the Vedic statement आयुर्वै घृतम् in his mind.

Oh goddess, now I want to offer honey to you. certainly people will derive lot of satisfaction on perceiving you, though you are basically beyond perception.

The poet next narrates the latter part of Pooja after Abhisheka;

अथ अभिषेकाद् अनन्तरं कुंकुमकेसरानुरञ्जित श्रीगन्ध द्रवानुलेपित सर्वाङ्गी श्रीशारदाम्बा आराधकैः निराजिताऽपि

1. *Ibid.* p. 12-13

संदर्शन दानेन भक्तलोकम् अन्वगृण्हात् शतरूद्रीय देवीसूक्तादि मंत्रपठनपूर्वकं निर्वर्तिते च अभिषेके दिव्याम्बर परिधापिता भूषणैः भूषितां मूर्तिं निमालय उत्सृष्टानन्दबाष्पधाराः देवीमित्थं वर्णया म्बभूवुः–

सर्वज्ञा सर्वशक्तिजगिद्दुदयकरी स्वात्मनैवाद्वितीया लीलामात्रेण कर्त्री
प्रकृतिरिति च या स्तूयते वेदवृन्दै।
सैवाहं माययैवारचित मिदमहं पालयामीति देवी स्वाङ्के बालां
निधाय प्रथयति जननी भक्तलोके स्वरूपम्॥
चराचर जगज्जनेः प्रथमजं हिरण्योदरम् प्रदर्श्य
जगदीशानां प्रथयितुं जने किन्विदम्।
शिशु शशिमुखं कनककान्ति मग्रेऽम्बिका
निधाय शयने सुखं स्मितमुखी शयानांप्रति॥

अथ धूप दीप नानाविध भक्ष्य भोज्यादि नैवेद्य फलताम्बूल नीराजन मंत्रपुष्पाञ्जलि प्रदक्षिण नमस्कारादीनां समर्पणेन आराधिता जगदम्बिका भक्तजनानां सुतानामिव संदर्शनामृतं संविभाजयन्तीव सर्वौः सादरं प्रेक्षमाणा च्छत्रचामराद्युपचारैः उपचर्यमाणा च नयनानन्दमातन्वती अतिमात्रं अदीव्यत॥[1]

After the abhisheka Sharadamba was anointed with Kunkum and scent. With the chanting of shatarudriya and devi Sukta as the concluding portion of the Abhisheka, Devi was described as follows;

She is all knowing, all powerful one and can create the world on account of her will. Here the poet seems to have the Brahma Sutra लोकवत्तु लीलाकैवल्यम् in his mind. Just as the mother protects her child by placing it in her lap, so does she protect the whole body.

She has also got the unique distinction of producing Hiranyagarbha the first and the foremost among the moveable as well as the immovable beings.

1. *Ibid.* p. 13-14

Then the goddess shawn brightly after she was also extended the chamara Seva by her Devotees and thus the whole sight was eye catching.

प्रतिपदुत्सववर्णनम्

As part of Pratipat, how Different scholars performed Different Parayanas is nicely narrated here;

अथ नवरात्र कल्प समुदीरित विद्यानेन वेदत्रयस्य गीतोपनिषद् ब्रह्मसूत्र भाष्याणां, श्रीमद्रामायण महाभारतादितिहासानां देवीभागवतादि महापुराणानां पारायणार्थम् आवृतेषु बहुषु दक्षेषु श्रीत्रियवरेषु ऋत्विक्षु गुर्वनुज्ञया समुपाक्रम्य स्वं स्वं पारायणं कृतवत्सु, भूषिताः सुवासिनीः हरिद्राकुंकुम वस्त्राभरण प्रसूनैः देवीमिव पर्यतोषयन्। तदनु च निखिल सुवासिनीः कुमारिकाभिः सह सहस्रशः पुरुषाश्च सर्वान् ऋत्विजः विद्यार्थिगणं च अमृतोपमैः नलपाकैः भोजयामासुः॥[1]

Then as part of the Navaratri Celebratings, there was the chanting of the three vedas in keeping with the tradition.

Some others were doing the Parayana of Bhagavad-gita, Upanishads, Ramayana, Mahabharata, Devi Bhaga-vata and Mahapuranas by the great scholars and on the other hand the womenfolk were doing Pooja to goddess by offering Saffron, Kunkum, Various Vastras and others. After this, there was meals extended to all the Suvasinis, Kumaris, Ṛtviks and others along with the students.

ARRIVAL OF ABHINAVA VIDYATEERHA SWAMIJI INTO THE TEMPLE

We have a graphic description of the arrival of Vidyateertha Swamiji here;

1. *Ibid.* p. 16

इतश्च पीताम्बरभासुराः करधृत पद्मराग मणिमालिकया देवीमनुराजम् अविरतं जपन्तः, अम्बिका मुख दत्त दृष्टयः, भासितलेखात्रयोद्भासित ललाटपट्टाः, अन्तेवसता च पट्टाम्बराच्छादित करावलम्बेन शनैरनुनीयमानाः, जोद्घुष्यमाण बिरूदावली घोष बृंहिताशान्तरालाः, राजहंसच्छदाभ श्वेतातपत्राभ्याम् उभयतः अनुसेव्यमानाः पार्श्वद्वयेपि तपः प्रभावोद्दीपित यशोधवालाभ्यां चामराभ्यां वीज्यमानाः। उशीरमय व्यजन वीजन दूरीकृत तपस्तापाः, शंख चक्रादि रेखा लक्षित रजतमय पादुकाभ्या पदसरोजे शनैः शनैः न्यस्यन्तः, श्रवण सुहित तूर्यनाद सेवा प्रसन्नीकृतानन चन्द्राः, गज तुरगच्छत्र चामर तोरणादिभिः पुरस्कृताः, करदीपिकाभिः प्रदर्षिताम्बरा प्रासादपथाः अनन्तश्रीविराजिताः बालगुखः श्रीममदभिनव विद्यातीर्थ यतिराजाः श्रीदेवीमन्दिरं किल समागमन्।[१]

Then entered the Junior Swamiji Sri Abhinava Vidyateertha who was wearing a pitambara, Who was incessantly doing the Japa of the goddess with the help of Padmaraga, whose face was concentrating on Ambika whose forehead had the three lines of sacred ashes, who was being followed by many followers, the different directions were reverberating with the uttering of the titles, on both the sides the devotees were fanning him with chamaras.

HOW THE SWAMIJIS WITNESSED THE PARAYANA

इत्थं च निवृत्ते देव्याः राजत रथोत्सवे, रथादवतीर्थ देवीं भद्रासने समुपवेश्य च, आराधकेषु गर्भगृहं प्रविष्टेषु, व्याख्यान सिंहासने देव्याः अभिमुख विभासमाने च बालजगद्गुरु सार्वभौमेषु विराजमानेषु, तच्चरणनलिनयोः स्वहित साष्टाङ्ग प्रणतयः लब्धानुमत यशश्च प्रागेव वृत्ताः पारायणाय ऋत्विजः सप्तशती स्तोत्रं सुस्वरं पठन्तः सवनिपि श्रोतॄन् पावयामासुः। उभयेऽपि गुरवः अम्बिकादत्त

1. *Ibid.* p. 16

दृष्टयः परमया भक्त्था नर्म कन्धराः सप्तशती स्तोत्रम् अशृण्वन्। चण्डिकास्तवस्यास्य श्रवणमात्रेणैव आबाल वर्षयिांसः सर्वेऽपि स्त्री पुंसाः अचिकिस्यादपि रोगान्निर्मुग्ताः। पराम् मुदम् अवात्नुवन्। यथाविधि विहितायां च चण्डिकास्तव पुस्तक सपर्यायाम्। अन्तः पुरान्तरित मूर्त्याः, देव्याः धूप दीप नैवेद्यादि सेवां व्यदधुः महता विभवेन श्रीमहागुरूपादाः॥[1]

In this way, when Devi's rathotasava was taking place, having got down from the chariot and having placed Devi in Bhadrasana and When the Aradhakas had entered sanctum sanctorum and when the junior pontiff was seated in front of the goddess in his Vyakhyana Simhasana the scholars offered their devotion at the lotus feat and then commenced the chanting of Sapta Shati. Both the pontiffs listened to this chanting with utmost attention. With just listening to it, the men old and young will be rid of their disease and get happiness. Then when the chanting came to a halt the elder Swamiji offered the worship of the goddess with Dhupa, Deepa and Niavedya.

The pooja of Swamiji to goddess is next narrated here;

ऽला लवङ्ग धनसार सुपूग नागवल्लीद्यैश्च सकदलैरपि स्वादुभूतम्।
ताम्बूलमात्मसुहितं कनके शृङ्के चक्षुर्विकर्षणकरे च मुदार्पिलंहि।
द्राक्षा दाड़िम मातुलुङ्ग कदली सेव्यानि दिव्यानि च स्वादिष्टानि
सुधारुचीनि जननी हस्तेंऽर्पितानि क्रमात्॥
तान्येतानि कुटुम्बिनां प्रतिगृहं चिन्ताफलावाज्ये।
नान्यस्मै सुफलाय, नित्यपरिलाम्बार्पितानि धृवम्।

1. *Ibid.* p. 17

सुवर्ण पुष्पाणि सुवर्ण धृष्टै देशेषु देशेषु गृहे गृहेच।
देव्यै मनोज्ञानि समर्पितानि भक्त्यां मुदा श्रीगुरुराजराजैः॥[1]

Swamiji offered Ela, Lavanga, Pooga Nagavalli, Tambula and others with all devotion. The various fruits like Grapes, Pomegranate, Banana etc. were gradually offered at the hands of the goddess.

Even the golden flowers brought from different households were also offered.

We have a beautiful Alliteration in the following three stanzas;

१. ऋष्यशृङ्ग पुरीश्वरी त्रिनयन ब्रह्मेन्द्रमुख्यैः स्तुते
ऋग्वेदादिभिरागमै मुनिवरै भक्त्या नुते भामिनि ।
ऋष्यशृङ्गवराश्रये विलसिते पीठे च भूषायिते
ऋग्वेदं शृणु विप्रवर्यपठितं देवि त्रयी सन्नुते ॥

२. यज्ञे यज्ञमये हुतेन हविषा संतार्यमाणे शुभे
यज्ञैज्ञनियमैः सुपूजितपदे स्वाध्याययज्ञैरपि ।
यज्ञेशाच्युत गधितांघ्रिकमले रक्ताब्ज रक्तप्रभे
यज्ञार्थं यजुरागमं शृणु मुदा संश्रावितं याजुषैः ॥

३. सामाम्नाय स्वरूपे त्रिदशमुनिगणैः सामभिर्गीयमाने
सामज्ञै र्भूमिदेवैरपि सततमिह स्तूयमाने गुणाढ्ये।
साम्न्यस्मिन् गीयमाने प्रतिपद जलित स्वोत्तमाङ्गे शुभाङ्गि
सामाम्नाय मुदा त्वं श्रुणु जननि पुरो गीयमाने द्विजेन्द्रैः॥[2]

Oh goddess belonging to the city of Rishya Sringa, one who has been adored by three Murthis Brahama, Vishnu and Siva, the sages have praised you reverentially in the Rigveda as well as various Agamas, you have adored the sacred seat of Rishya Sringa.

---

1. *Ibid.* p. 18
2. *Ibid.* p. 18-19

Please listen to the chanting of Rigveda by Brahmins.

Oh goddess, Please listen to Yajurveda by which the offerings ore offered to fire at the time of the performance of a sacrifice. Oh red complexioned one, you have been the very incarnation of the sacrifice.

Oh goddess kindly perceive the chanting of Samaveda as you are the very incarnation of Sama. This reminds us of the statement of Bhagavad Gita; वेदानां सामवेदोस्मि।

Next, the author gives out the final prayer offered to goddess for the well being of humanity before the conclusion;

स्वस्ति मंत्रार्थाः सत्याः सफलाः संस्त्विति महान्तोऽनुगृण्हन्तु। अनेन शरन्नवरात्रोत्सवे अनुष्ठित निखिलागम पुराणेतिहास पारायणेन सवनत्रय समर्हणेन विशेषतः ब्राह्मण सुवासिनी समाराधितेन नक्तं तन स्यन्दनोत्सव सप्तशतीस्तव श्रवण दीपाराधनादि कैंकर्याचरणेन, शतचण्डी यागेन च यथाविधि समाचरितेन, अन्यैश्च नित्योत्सव, पक्षोत्सव, मासोत्सव, संवत्सरोत्सवैः श्री महामयी महालक्ष्मी महासरस्वत्यात्मिका श्री देवी शारदाम्बा सुप्रीता सुप्रसन्ना वरदा ब्रह्म क्षत्र वैश्य शूद्राणां चतुर्णानपि वर्णानाम्, शैव, वैष्णव, शाक्त सौर कापालिक गाणपत्यानां षणमताविष्ट चेतसां क्षेमस्थैर्यवीर्य विजयामायुरारोग्य ऽेश्वर्याद्यष्टैश्वर्यप्रदा भूयादिति महान्तोऽनुगृण्हन्तु।[1]

The Swasti Mantras may it be Truth and may it yield fruit-let the people approve this with the chanting of the Vadas, and the performance of Nityopasana, Pakshopasana, Masopasana, Samvatsaropasana may the goddess Sharada who is the combination of Mahakali, Mahalaksnmi and Maha Saraswathi be pleased and

1. *Ibid.* p. 20

confer well being, victory, longevity, health and wealth on all the fourfold caste namely Brahman, Kshatriya, Vaishya and Shudra from one end to the other.

ROUTINE FROM SECOND DAY ONWARDS

प्रतिपदीव द्वितीयादि चतुर्थ्यान्तासु तिथिषु दिवा ऋवसु यथापूर्वं वेदेतिहास पुराणादि पारायणम् अनुतिष्ठत्सु। सवनद्वय सपर्यायां यथागमं निर्वर्तितायां, ब्राह्मण सुवासिनी समाराधन भोजनादिषु च ससुखवृत्तेषु, तृतीयसवानारम्भे च देव्याः उत्सवे भक्तजनैः विभवेन अनुष्ठिते नक्तं श्री गुरुपादाः सह शिष्यैः बाल गुरुपादैः वाद्यघोष पुरस्सरं देव्यालयं प्रविश्य यथापूर्वं रजतमय स्यन्दनीत्सवम् अतिवेल प्रमोदजनन दर्शं दर्शं समुद्रिक्त हर्षकञ्चकित, रजतमय व्याख्यान सिंहासने भक्तकिङ्करैः शनैः सप्तवेशिताः आराध नेन विप्रवर्येण सुस्वरम् उच्चकैः सप्तशती स्तवम् देव्यामेव दत्त दृष्टयः, समन्ततः समुपविष्टैः सभक्तिश्रद्धं विनयावनमीकृत कन्ध रैः सर्वैरपि नर नारी जनैः सह अश्टण्वन्। अथ च धूप दीप नैवेद्यान्तेषु उपचारेषु यथाविभवं चरितेषु जवनिकान्तरित मूर्तिं देवीं द्रष्टुकामाः समाजिकाः इव सर्वेऽपि अहमहमिकया दण्डिपुरुषेण निवार्यमाणाः अपि पुरः प्रसृत कन्धराः, जवनिकायां अपसारितायां संबिभ्रतीं पञ्चभिः आरर्तिकैः नीराज्यमानां सादरं दृग्भिः निपीय अमृतान्धसा अमृतमपि तुच्छीकुर्वन्तिः विस्मृतात्मानः हर्षातिरेकेण अनृत्यन्। ऽवमेव देवी स्वरूपं चिन्तयन्तः तिथित्रयमपि सुखेन अत्यवाहयन्॥[1]

Like the pratipat from the second to the fourth day also as before the priests during the day time did the parayana of Vedas, Itihasas, Puranas and the feeding of the Brahmins and Suvasinis followed afternoon and night and with the commencement of the·third day,

1. *Ibid.* p. 21

the Senior Pontiff entered the temple along with the Junior pontiff in accompaniment of the different auspicious sounds.

The Ritviks started chanting Saptashati loudly which was heard by one and all assembled there with utmost reverence.

Then the Dhupa, Deepa and Naivedaya followed as before but the people were all along curious to see the face of goddess which was covered with veil but the security guard was there to control them from rushing forward with his stick and their having had the Dasrhan of the goddess the devotees danced in joy.

The beauty of the goddess is pen pictured nere;

वाचेन्दु लेखाकृत शीर्षभूषा सौम्या त्रिनेत्रां चर्म भूषाम्।
वरं त्रिशूलं परशुं च खड्गं करैर्दधानां हृदये निचिक्युः॥
यञ्चच्चन्दर कोटि भासुरतरं पिच्छं प्रसर्यामितः।
नृत्यं कुर्वंति भोगियोग निहित स्वांघ्रिद्वये माद्यति।
वर्णैः पञ्चभिरञ्चिताङ्गः मधुरैर्दिव्ये मयूरे मुदा।
कौमारीं च कृतासनां स्मितमुखीमम्बामपश्यन्मुदा॥[१]

Then as usual the Astavadhana was offered and the uttara Nirajana was given to god but the people who were unable to leave the temple had to go to their houses much against their will for doing service to the old parents and to take care of the young ones.

ROUTINE FROM THE FIFTH DAY TO NINTH DAY CELEBRATIONS

How the morning functions began is pen pictured here;

---

1. *Ibid.* p. 22

अग्रे करिण्यो तुरगौ च भूषा विभूषितौ चामर आतपत्रम्।
सुतोरणं वाद्यविधाः विचित्रः सूर्यप्रभा भास्वर दीपिकाश्च॥
पश्चाच्च देव्याः स्तुतिपाठकाश्च भक्ता जनन्याः यजनेऽनुरक्त।
इत्येवमाद्यैर्विभिवैर्मनोज्ञैः महोत्सवो वीथि चतुष्टयेऽभूत॥
तथा यथापूर्व विद्यानमेते सुमन्दिर सद्गुखोऽभिगक्य।
रथोत्सवं सप्तशती स्तुतीनां पाठं च सर्वं निखर्तयंश्च॥[1]

The elephants in the front, this being followed by the horses and then the people with chamaras in their hands and then the People chanting the praises of the goddess, the devotees singing Bhajana like this the festivities were carried out in all the main roads. Infront of the pontiffs and before the scholars chanted the saptashati.

Nest we have the offerings to Goddess;

तदनु च श्रीगुरुपादानाभिः अध्यक्षमेव ऋत्विग्भिः
सह आचार्यः उत्तिष्ठन् पूर्णाहुतिमंत्रमुञ्चरन्।
आहुतिद्रव्याणि सर्वाण्यपि ऽाकैकशः सुचिरं
श्रीचण्डिका परितृत्यये होमकुण्डे काली कराली
प्रमुख लेलियमान जिह्वाभिः सप्तभिः
समुज्चलति हव्यवाहे "न मम" इत्यनुसन्दधानः प्राक्षिपत्।[1]

Then in the guidance of Swamiji the various priests got up and by Chanting the Mantra of Poornaahuti, offered all the ingredients into the fire, when the seven tongues of the fire were active in devouring it. The seven tongues mentioned here reminds us of the following mantra of Mandakopanishad;

काली कराली च मनोजवा च सुलोहिता याच सुधूम्रवर्णा।
स्फुलिङ्गिनी विश्वरुची च देवी लेलायमाना इति सप्तजिह्वाः॥

---

1. *Ibid.* p. 24

The food prepared on this occasion is graphically presented here;

अहो नु खलु व्यायाम विस्तरेषु वर्धमानकेषु सुमल्लिकाकुसुम-राशयः इव अन्नराशंयः चक्षुर्मनो हारिणः, पुरुष प्रमाणेषु भाजनेषु रस सूप तेमन प्रभृतयः रसोत्तरा व्यञ्जन विशेषाः बलाद् घ्राणमाकर्षन्ति रुग्णानामपि रसनेन्द्रिय जिह्वा निक्तता दूरीकरणानि उपसेचनानि। गोधूम पायसं हि मधुरतरैः केसरैः सुरभीकृतं पुट पात्र पेयं पुरुषायामपात्रेषु संपूरितम् आस्वादनाय सर्वेषामपि जिह्वाः चापलयति।[1]

In the places of doing exercises the heaps of rice were appearing as though they were jasmine flowers spread there, the vessels in which the rice was prepared was on par with people in their size. There was different food items whose smell the nose perceived. The food items served as though to give taste even to the diseased people whose tongue would have lost all taste. The Payasa made on that occasion which was applied with saffron used to captivate the tongue of everyone.

Next we have narration of Rathotasva;

भद्रासनाधिष्ठित मूर्तिमम्बां भद्रकरी भूषण भूषिताङ्गीम् भद्रातपत्रेण निषेव्यमाणां समूह्यमानां वरयात्ययाने। वेणुनादसदृशैः श्रुतिसौख्यैः वाद्यघोषचिययैरतिपेलम् वीचितल्य सरल स्वर भङ्गैः नैकरागलहरी प्लवमानैः॥ भाकृ गर्भ निविष्टैः पूरिताविल दिशान्तर गर्भैः। दुन्दुभिहवानिमिस्त्सवे तथा डिडिम प्रभृतिनिस्वनैश्चिरम्। सर्वतोऽपि पशुवत् परिमूषः निर्विच्चेष्टितपादाः शिशवोऽपि लीन नौज हृदया भुदम्ब्रधौ श्लाधनाय तलदात्मशिरस्काः॥[2]

The goddess was seated in her posture who is capable of bestowing auspiciousness, on others and who is endowed with various ornaments and who has been fanned by the auspicious umbrellas. Here we have a fine आदिप्रास।

1. *Ibid.* p. 26
2. *Ibid.* p. 27

The chanting of the vedas which resembled the playing on the lute, the sound of the different auspicious organs appeared as though different melodious waves put into one.

Everywhere people were dumb founded including the children. The only movement which could be seen was the moving of the head.

A fine विराधाभासालंकार could be noticed here.

अथ च सकलसंयमि सार्वभौम मुकुटायमानाः, मुकरानल कृताना अपि आखण्डित ब्रह्मचर्य तेजोमय मुकुटोज्वलाननाः, दूरीकृत मुक्ताहारा अपि अरीकृत व्रत मुक्ताहाराः, परित्यक्त पीताम्बरा अपि अपरित्यक्त पीताम्बराः, परिहृत सिंहासनारोहणाः अपि अपरिहतसिंहासनाः। जन्मना कलियुगीना अपि कर्मणा कृतयुगीनाः। देवी वशीकृतस्वात्मनोऽपि वशीकृत देव्यात्मानः। विधूतच्छत्रचामरा अपि असि अविधूतगुरुपादकाच्छत्रचामराः, सन्यस्त सकलकमणिोऽपि असन्यस्त लोककल्याण कमणिः, त्यक्सकलैश्वर्या अपि अपरित्यक्त निखिलैश्वर्याः, सर्वतो विरक्ता अपि सनातन धर्मनुरक्ताः, धृत काषायाम्बराः, परिपदकाषायाः, रूद्राक्षमालाधारिणः, भस्म त्रिपुण्ड्र रेखोद्भासित फालार्द्रचन्द्राः, चन्द्रमौलीश्वरापरावताराः गीयमान परमहंस परिव्राजरत्यादि विरुदावली विराजमानाः श्रीजगद्गुरू महाराजाः प्रासादगर्भगृहं प्रविश्य नक्तं देव्याः आराधनम् आरभन्त॥[१]

Then they were like the supreme among those who had self restraint, though they had not adored themselves their head with a crown still they were adored on account of the penance being performed, though they had abandoned pitambara still they were wearing pitambara as it were, though they were not ascending the throne, still they had ascended the one though they were born in Kali age, by their birth they

1. *Ibid.* p. 28

were in Krita age, though they had abandoned chamaras still their devotees had not abandoned it, though they had abandond Karma still they were doing the useful Karmas for the sake of the people, though they had renunciated everything, still they were attached to the Sanatana Dharma, they were wearing ochre robes, rosaries, their forehead was covered by the Tripumdra and were really the incarnations of Lord chandra-mouliswara who were being welcomed with titles, enterd the Swamijis and started doing the Pooja to the goddess during the night.

We have a fine alliteration here;

दुर्गाणां तरणे तटीं भजनतो लभ्या चिरं ध्यायिनाम् दुर्दर्शामपि योगिनां भगवतीं सिंहासनिष्ठाम् नताम्। दुर्गां दुगर्ति दारणैक करुणा पूर्णात्मि दृष्टिंनतेरां दृष्ट्वैवात्मशरांसि भक्तिशयतः सर्वेप्यधोऽनामयन्॥[१]

The famous statement of Dakshinamurthi Stortra गुरोस्तु मौनव्याख्यानं शिष्यास्तु छिन्नसंशयाः seems to have inspired the poet here;

पद्मासनस्था वटवृक्षसमूले चिन्मुदया मुद्रित दक्षहस्ता।
मौनेन शिष्यान् प्रतिबोधयन्ती श्रीदक्षिणामूर्तितनुर्बभासे॥[२]

The work comes to an end with a fine alliteration;

जयतु जयतु देवी शारदाम्बा जगत्याम्
जयतु जयतु नित्यं सद्गुरुर्नशिचिराय।
जयतु जयतु धर्मो चोक्कल्याणकारी
जयतु जयतु शश्वद् दक्षिणाम्नायपीठम्॥[३]

Thus Sharannavaratrotsava Champu is an authentic account of the Navaratri festival in Sringeri for which

1. *Ibid.* p. 28
2. *Ibid.* p. 30
3. *Ibid.* p. 35

the author Vidvan K.Krishna Jios was an eye witness on inumberable occasions. The work has beautiful alankaras like Malopama, Anuprasa, Virodhabhasa, and so on. The philosophical acumen of the poet could be gleaned through then and there in the work in which he is a great master. (He is the professor of Advaita Vedanta in the Shankara Mutt, Bangalore). Thus the work could be termed as a Bhakti Kavya as the author himself admitts before the commencement of the work. The author had the blessings of both the pontiffs Chandrasekhara Bharathi Swamiji as well as Abhinava Vidyateertha Swamiji who have honoured the poet with the title pandita pravara from their Mutt. The work serves the purpose of a historical account as well as a eminent travelogue and hence could be termed as a multi purpose Kavya and a source book on Sringeri.

4

SRI RAGHAVENDRA GURUSARVABOUMA SAPTARATROSAVA CHAMPU PANHAMUKHI RAGHAVENDRACHARYA-1977

Sri Raghavendra Gurusarvabhouma Saptaratrotsava Champu is one of the two Champus written by Panchamukhi Raghavendracharya and published by the author himself from Dharwar in the year 1977 with financial assistance from the ministry of education and social welfare, government of India, New Delhi. The present work is unique in many respects. It conforms to the admixture of prose and poetry in high classical style being divided into fourteen Ullasas, the work describes also the events of the seven days of the festival like the bath of the pilgrims in the river, hallowed by the presence of the swamiji Sri Suyameendrateertha the promoter and director of the whole festival, the worship of Sri Raghavendra Swamigal by ablution, decoration lamps and Hastodaka to the saint, freeing of the Brahmins and thousands of visiting devotees as well as the Vahanotsava and Rathotsava festival of specified days according to the usual custom. In all the vivid descriptions of the events emphasis is laid on their cultural and spiritual aspects thereby highlighting the greatness of Indian Traditional Values in general.

The new elements introduced in the champu include series of lectures by pandits and specified scholars on important problems of philosophy in easy readable style so as to be intelligible to the common man, such as conference of haridasas, congregation of poets and pandits, Examination of students in Sastras which is an intellectual and a cultural meal offered to the pilgrims. The festival is packed with various academic programmes of living interest in which the pilgrims find perenninal joy and inspiration for ennobling their lives. The corputitior competition of talents described in the twelfth and thirteenth ullasas in the instantaneous compositions of poems highly embellished with classical style of expression and thought, adds to the champu the a of Mahakavya which according to the traditional definition should contain the description of mountains, ocean, the seasons, river, etc.

Another unique feature of the work is the inclusion of the Dramas or narrative plays namely, मध्वविजयनाटक, प्रह्लादवरद नरसिंहप्रादुर्भाव नाटक, गुरूराजवैभवनाटक relating to the life of Sri Raghavendra Teertha in his present and former a vataras. These are designed to interest the visitors of the festivals in the great achievement of the Avataras of the God and his messengers the vibhuti for the uplift of mankind.

Each of the Ullasas have even given an appropriate

name like चम्पूग्रथने गुरुप्रेरणा the inspiration of the greaty masters in the composition of the champu work, गुरुसार्वभौमाणां पूर्वावतार कथाविलासा:, the previous incarnation of great masters, श्रीगुरुसार्वभौमाणां अवतारकथामृतम् the incarnation of the great masters, which continue in the fifth and the sixth ullasas also, the seventh ullasa narrates the first daty festivities under a weaklong festivity श्रीगुरुसार्वभौम सप्तरात्रोत्सवे प्रथमदिनोत्सव:, eighth ullasa narates the second day festivities nimth ullasa depicts the third day festivities श्रीगुरुसार्वभौम साप्नरात्रोत्सवे द्वितीय दिनोत्सव: the tenth ullasa portrays the fourth day festivities, श्रीगुरुसार्वभौम सप्तरात्रोत्सवे तृतीयदिनोत्सव:, the eleventh ullasa delineates the fifth day festivities श्रीगुरुसार्वभौम सप्तरात्रोत्सवे पंचमदिनोत्सव:, the twelfth ullasa narrates the seventh eay festivities श्रीगुरुसार्वभौम सप्तरात्रोत्सवे षष्ठ दिनोत्सव:, and the fourteenth ullasa portrays the vision of pranadeva and offering the champu श्रीपंचमुखी प्राणदेवसन्दर्शनं चम्पूसमर्पणं च।

In this background, an attempt is made in the following pages to analyse the work as a sample survey.

चम्पूग्रथनेगुरुप्रेरणा

The first forty two stanzas depict the inspiration derived from various Gods and masters like Goddess Lakshmi, Hari, vedavyasa, Poornaprajna, Krishna, Sripadaraja, Vyasateertha, Vadiraja, Vijayendra Teertha, Sri Raghavendra and so on. The following prose passage clarifies the intention of poet in composition to this work;

अयमहमाज्ञतोऽस्मि कर्मन्दिवरेण निस्तद्रसान्द्र भक्तिभार भासुरेण श्रीसुधीन्द्रसुतसेवकेन श्रीसुयमींन्द्रयमीन्द्रेण श्रीसुजयीन्द्रगुरूलालित

पदपङ्क्जेनाहूय मया गुरूसेवा समनुष्ठेया ललितपदविन्यास विकस्वरेण शब्दार्थालकार निपयेन नवरसनिस्यन्दिना वाक्कुसुम गुच्छेन प्रबन्थेन भक्तितुलसीदाम निबन, आगामिन्याराधन महोत्सवे निलिंपबर्योत्सवे परिशन्निर्यच्चित्सव इतिं गुवज्ञितिरस्करणं ननु महदनर्थ परंपराङ्गीकरणम्। अत उद्यम्यते अचिराद्यथा बुद्धिविभवं प्रबन्ध-रचनाचातुरी निचयाय॥[१]

I have been instructed by Sage Suyamindra that I have to compose a work with nicely balanced words in champu style endowed with beautiful alankaras generating a new Rasa in the form of a garland made out of Tulasi and it should be ofiered at the ensuing function. for which we have a reference in the last Ullasa hence the author has maintained the dictum; उपक्रमोपसंहारे ऽाक्वाग्यता To violate the orders of the masters will lead to terrible calamities. Hence I commence this work immediately keeping in mind my limitations.

SECOND CHAPTER- THE BERTH OF PRAHLADA AND HIS UNFLINCHING DEVOTION TO GOD

दैवदुर्विहतौ जयविजयो प्रथमे जन्मनि हिरण्यकशिपुः हिरण्याक्ष इति प्रथितपराक्रमों चण्डशासनौ दैत्यापसदावभूताम्। हिरण्यकशिपोः कयाधूपरिग्रहे साधुजन निपशनिं ज्ञानभक्तिदयासांत्यादि सद्गुधणाना-मुत्पत्तिस्थानं धैर्यस्थैर्ययोर्जन्मभूमिः त्यागदामदमाना माकरः, देवैरपि निसर्गशिुभिः अनुकरणीयत्वेन श्लाघितसत्वः शक्तित्रयसंपन्नः प्रह्लाद इति प्रथितः सुतः सक्ल सज्जनानाह्लादयन् अनवद्य पुण्यमुहूर्ते सरगुरुभाने जनिमवाप.... आश्रम परिसरेषु निवसन्तः निसर्गशत्रवः मार्जारमूषकाः शार्दूलगावः सिंहकरिहरिणाः अदृष्टभूतपूर्वं विचित्रं स्नेहरसमाविष्कुर्वनः परस्परसङ्गताः क्रीड़न्तिस्म॥[२]

---

1. Sri Raghavendra Gurusa Vabhouma Saptaratrotsava Champu- Panchamukhi Raghavendracharya-Dharwar. 1977. p. 5.
2. *Ibid.* p. II.12

Jaya and Vijaya in their former birth were born as Hiranya Kashipu and Hiranyaksha who were a menace to the world. Hiranya kashipu on marrying Kayadhu got a son named prahlada who was a model to all the saints, an abode of knowledge, devotion, renunciation, courage, resoluteness whose sativik temperament was initiated even those who had mutual animosity on an auspicious occasion. The animals with mutual animosity like the rat and the cat, the cow and the tiger, the lion and the deer exhibited mutual friendship which was unhead of.

The same description could be noticed in Bana's kadambari also in depicting the hermitage of Jabali.

The unflinching devotion of Prahlada is nicely narrated here;

न कदापि मयि कामसंरोहः पोषमुपयातु। मम अक्षिणी पुण्डरीकाक्षमक्षमे भूयास्ताम्। पादौ तन्मन्दिरप्राप्तौ व्यापृतौ हस्तौ तन्मूर्तिसपर्यायां च सज्जेताम्। घ्राणः तद्वक्षस्थलाश्रित श्रीवत्स व्यासङ्गाद्यासित परिमलित कुसुममञ्जरी माघ्रयीं घृणानिधिशरणमातनोतु। जिह्वापि तच्छेषरता स्वादने तन्नामगणने च रमताम्। किं बहुना, ममात्मैव अनिभृतं तच्चरणनलिनपुरेऽनिमित्तहस्तेन समर्पित इति सगद्गदमुद्गिरन् नयनाश्रुधारया तत्पादपदये सिञ्चन् आत्मन्यात्मानं धारयंस्तूष्णीं बभूव काञ्चिदनेहस्तम्।[1]

At no Point of time may I get lust. Let my hands offer Pooja to him. Let my nose smell the fragrant flowers through which the neck of the Lord is adored. Let my tongue chant his name. what to say more, I have offered my entire personality at his lostus feet and as and when he was telling this, his throat became

1. *Ibid.* p. 17

choked and tears rolled down his cheeks and he became quiet.

कणटिकविद्यासिंहासनाधीश्वरः व्यासयोगीश्वरः

First the author gives a background to Bharatha here;

अस्ति प्रत्यस्तमितमस्ततिप्रसरे सत्वोर्जिताश्वर धौर्य विरावित निद्रालुकद्र समुत्थाव्रद्रोरगरक्षोगणे भूसुर वारासार्दित सुरेन्द्रसंपदकूपरे हिमानीपति गिरिपुरारोघ धित्यके यक्षरक्षकिन्नरोरग गन्धर्वाप्सरोगण कलाप्रयोग क्रीड़ाभूमौ भरतवर्षे भरतखण्डे जम्बूद्वीपे भारतं नाम पुण्यतमं क्षेत्रम्।।[१]

On the different peaks of Himalayas we have various people like Yaksha, Rakshsa, Kinnara, Gaṅdharva, Apsaras and other in the Bharatha kanda Jambu dweepa a holy pilgrimage known as Bharatha.

Then the author gives a fitting introduction to Karnataka;

तत्र सौवर्णांशुलीयक पिद्यारक्त स्फुरन्मणिरिव गमलोदर मृदुमृणालमिव पुण्डरीकगर्भभार वत्कर्णिकावत गैवणिवाणी ब्रह्माणी-कण्ठमणिरिव भारतवर्ष भूषायमाणो भारतभानिनीभाम पोष कुन्तलायमान कुतल विषयप्ररंध्य्रः कर्णपूर इव कर्णाटकजनपद लवणोपहयमासो प्रथमापोदानं अगस्त्येन शिरवरिन्यताङ्गुलि न्यगरेणा-वभुग्नशीर्षस्य विद्यादेः दक्षिणतः नदीनिर्झारवापीकूप तटाकरजलशयैः वनोपवनारामरविहार क्रीड़ाभूमिभिः पर्वर्ताद्रशिलोच्च पादि शिखरिभिः कृष्णरक्तसैकत प्रकारार्थिः उर्वराथिः वन्यमृगसिंह शार्दूल हरिणहरिणी भूयिष्ठाभिः अरुणभूमिभिश्च समलंकृतः प्रकामं शरान्यते।[२]

1. *Ibid.* p. 19
2. *Ibid.* p., 19.20

There like the tender lotus fibres the Sanskrit language as though an ear ornament to the beautiful maidens exist a region known as Karnataka wherein Agastya the revered sage drank the entire ocean for the first time, wherein is situated the Vindhya Mountains to the South and we have abundance of rivers, rivulets, waterfalls, forests, gardens and places of relaxation and in the forests we have number of wild animals like Lion, Tiger and others.

THE BIRTH OF VYASATEERTHA

ऽवं गुणगणैलंकृते कर्णाटकजनपदे जगतः मूर्धायमानः दार्शनिकमौलिमणिः श्रीव्यासतीर्थगुरूसार्वभौमः बन्नूरुग्रामे सदाचारतपः पूते निञतान्तपान्ते ब्राद्धणकुले अवातरत्।[1]

In the place Karnataka which is endowed with precious qualifies, which has given birth to many Philosophers was born Sri Vyhasateertna to a chaste Brahmin couple in a village called Bannuru.

THE BIRTH OF VYASATEERTHA-PEOPLE'S REACTION

महान्खलु प्रमोदः समजनि समेषां सत्वप्रधानानां जनानां यत ज्ञानाज्ञानविवेकलिकले कलिकालकालिम्ना धर्मात्पथः प्रत्युते समये समग्रानुग्रह विधाता संशयच्छेत्रा निगूढ़ं तत्वद्वप्रदेष्टा लोकोत्तरप्रज्ञः प्रेक्षावान्गुरु जिज्ञासुभिः पुरः पथावशनिन विद्वेलतित्रैः तितरामीत्सितोऽभवत्। सच तादृशो वेत्ता शीर्षण्यजन कृत सुकृतपरिपाकेन विशेषतः परमात्मनः श्रीहरेः परमप्रसादेनैव श्री व्यासतीर्थ नाम्ना यतिवरेण्येन प्रतिनिधीकृतः।[2]

For all the good people it caused a great delight

1. *Ibid.* p. 20
2. *Ibid.* p. 20

when in Kali Age the Dharma was in its lowest ebb, to bless everyone, to remove the doubts of the people, to preach the highest philosophy, the torch bearer for the people who want to know about God was represented in the form of Vyasateertha who was born with the grace of Sri Hari.

How even the animals were filled with joy at the birth of Vyasateertha is nicely brought out here;

मयूराः शिखण्डैः पिच्छभारैः सुवर्णैः
रनृत्यन् समंतदृंश वाद्यैररण्ये।
पिकाद्या विहङ्गा हर्षगानं व्यतन्वन्
यदा व्यासराजः सपृथिव्यां बभूव॥[१]

The peacocks opened their feathers and danced in delight in the forest and the parrots welcomed his birth by a joyous song.

FOURTH FIFTH AND SIXTH CHAPTERS-THE AVATARA OF THE VARIOUS GURUS

One can note a nice Malopama in the following passage;

ततः पचेलिमाःऽखिलनिलिम्प कलापोषसुषमिते गर्भे ज्योनिर्गणप्रगुण गुणगणिते लवनाड़ी दलशुङ्गिसंस्हते समये मंगलासंगोत्रद्रगदिने सुमुहूर्ते सा कुलीनललना गोषाम्बिका पूर्वेन्दुमिव सिन्धुवेला प्रसृमर तेजः सारं वामनमिव कश्यपदयिता अदितिः हिरण्यकश्यपजयवधूः कयाधूः निर्धूतमोहं प्रह्लादमिव भीमनादं भीमसेनमिव पाण्डुदयिता कुन्ती भागवतमिव आम्नायार्थसारं श्रत्यङ्गना प्रसुषुवेऽलौकिकतेजोभूतं तेजस्विनं अर्भकं भविष्यज्जगद्गुरूं महानुभावम्।[२]

---

1. *Ibid.* p. 20
2. *Ibid.* p. 41

The prowess of that boy Venratanatha is graphically portrayed here;

कृतचूड़ाकर्मा काकपक्षधरः कलहंसकण्ठः निसर्गदृढ़ पुष्टगरिष्ठ-गात्रेऽयं बालः क्रमेण गायत्रीमंत्रोपदेशकारी संवृत्तः। परंपरागतविधया गृह ऽव लिपिपरिचयं लघुकाव्यपठनं बाललोकमलिलीलासुलभं भारत भागवत रामायण कथासंकथनकौशलं चाधीतवान् पितृपादसन्नि-धाने। अष्टमेवर्षे कृतोपनयनः स्वाध्याय अध्ययने निबद्दचित्तः त्रिकालसंद्यााया निकायादि कर्मकलापाननुतिष्ठान् चतुर्वेदान्साङ्गान् कण्ठपाठेन स्वायकृतवान्। अनायासेन हस्तासात्कृतचतुर्वेद वेदराशिः ब्राह्मणकारण्यकोपनिषदादि वाङ्मयं अनायासेन कण्ठेऽक्रोत् अकुण्ठधिषणः वेंक्टनाथः॥[१]

After the choodakarna, that now who was made strong by nature with a melodious voice became fit. for the initiation of Gayatri. In a traditional way in his house he had the initial training of reading and writing and gradually mastered Bharatha, Bhagavatha, Ramayana. In the eighth year he was initiated and having practiced Sandhya thrice a day he memorised all the four vedas. Then Venkatanatha also mastered the various accessories of Vedas like Brahmanas, Aranyaras and Upanishads.

RAGHAVENDRA GURU

Nest we have a pen picture of the greatness of Raghavendra Guru;

जानीध्वं मम शिष्यका यतिवरः श्रीराघवेन्द्रो गुरूः
देवांशः स महीतले विजयते माध्वाब्धिजैवातृकः।
शास्त्रे देवगुरूः सतां हितगुरूः श्रीकृष्णसाक्षात्करूः
तद्भक्तः सुतरां कलावनुवृतः कृष्णस्य साक्षी हरिः।

1. *Ibid.* p. 43

राघवेन्द्र गुरुराट् प्रगीयते दैत्यसूनुखतीर्ण इत्यलम्
प्राग् बभूव सन्तु व्यासतीर्थ भियाहतः सकलसूरिथिर्मुदा।
वन्ध गष पृथबुद्धिवल्लभः वैष्णवैरमल बृद्धिभिर्गुरुः॥
नैव देवतकुलावतंसको सिद्धवृतिविषयी नृणां भवेत्॥

Please consider this Raghavendra Guru as an incarnation of Madhwa. In the Sastras he is like Brihaspati, he is the bestower of goodness for the incarnation of Prahlada the son of Hirang Kashipu. In his privious birth he was born as Vyasateertha.

गुरुसार्वभौम सजरात्रोत्सवे प्रथमदिनोत्सवः

The Pooja offered by Swamiji to Moola Rama is graphicaily portrayed here;

श्रीपादाः गन्धाक्षतार्पणादि पूजामर्पयित्वा प्रत्यग्रानीत कोमलतुलसीदलैः सजाति केतरीमल्लिका सुमहारैः सुमनोहरैः समर्चतः ब्रह्मसूत्राणि विष्णुसहस्रनामानि च पठन्तः श्रीमूलराम दिग्विजयराम जयरामप्रतिमाः सादरभक्ति भासुर स्तोत्रपदैः स्तुवंतः शिष्यवृन्दैः मंत्रपाठकैः उच्चैः स्वरेण गायद्भिः साकं महादामांद मर मन्वभिवना गद्ग दस्वरेण हर्षनिर्भरेण। तदर्वाक् परिमल धूमाघ्राणनेन देवतामुख विकासमवलोकयन्तः दीपावलीं पार्श्वयोः प्रज्वाल्य क्षुभदयमोन्य लेद्धपेयापिकं चतुर्विधान्न समृष्टमार्णयामासुः द्वादशस्तोत्रपठन पुरस्सरं। नारायणप्रणवमूलमंत्रान् जपित्वा दृष्टिदोषविद्यातार्थं त्रिवारं द्वांशख-भ्रमणेन शंखोदकं पात्रान्तरं निधाय रमाब्रद्धादि देवताश्ल परिवारत्वेन पूजयित्वा नैवेघशेषं समर्पयामासुः॥[1]

Then Swamiji with Gandha and Akshata performed Pooja with the help of Tulasi, Ketaki, Mallika garlands. Then followed the devotees who were reciting Brahma Sutras, Vishnu Sahasranama and carried the idols of Sri Moola Rama, Digvijaya Rama and Jaya Rama. Then

1. *Ibid.* p. 7.

the sacred Dhoopa and Deepa was offered and the fourfold food was offered to god as Naivedya. Then the oola antras of Narayana pranava was recited and the water was poured thrice to avoid inauspiciousness and gradually the family deities Rama, Brahma were invoked and thus Naivedya was completed.

After this, there was a discourse on Veda Nityatva.

श्रीगुरुसार्वभौम सजरात्रोत्सवे द्वितीयदिनोत्सवः

श्रीपादास्तु प्रत्यूषसि यथाविधि निष्पाद्य श्रीगुरुराङ्दर्शनस्तवनपुरः कार्यानुष्ठानासिनुज्ञायाज्यनादिकर्मा विदातं हंसमंत्रनारायण कृष्ण वासुदेव धन्वन्तरि प्रभृतिमंत्र विशेषान् महामंत्रानपि नियतसंख्यया जपित्वा प्रतिमंत्र कलृत्लसंख्यया तर्पणदिकं दत्वा प्रातराह्निकं पूरयामासुः॥[1]

Then the प्रमाणलक्षणोपन्यास is dealt at length with all the arguments and counter arguments as it is one of the basics of Dvaita Vedanta.

After this Sumadhva Vijaya Nataka is enacted.

श्रीगुसार्वभौम सप्तरात्रोत्सवे तृतीयदिनोत्सवः

UNDER the auspices of श्रीमत्समीरमयसंवर्धिनी सभा how the intellectual devates es were held on various sastraic elements is portrayed here;

The Ultimate Siddhanta of Dwaita Vadanta is nicely narrated in the following stanza;

श्रीमन्मध्वमते हरिः परतरः सन्यं जगत्तत्ववर्ता
भेदो जीवगणा हेररनुचराः नीचोच्चभावं गताः।
मुक्तिर्नैज सुखानुभूतिरमला भग्तिश्च तत्साधनम्
ह्यक्षादित्रितयं प्रमाणमखिलाम्नायैक वेद्योहरिः॥[2]

1. *Ibid.* p. 95
2. *Ibid.* p. 135

In the Siddhanta of adhwa, Hari is the highest, the world is real and the Jivas who are the followers of Hari are classified according to their merits. Salvation is the only natural happiness and to get that the means is Devotion. There are only three pramanas and Hari could be known only through Vedas.

This is followed by Haridasa pausrad and the enactment of श्रीपह्लादवरद नृसिंह प्राद्रर्थावनाटकम्

श्रीगुरुसार्वभौम सप्नरात्रोत्पले चतुर्थीदिनोत्सवः

We can note the highest philosophy in the following passage;

दुर्लभं मानुषं जन्म तदप्यध्रुवमर्थदम्। अतः ऽेन्द्रियकं सुखं दुःम्बक्याज्यमेव। नश्वरस्य क्षणमात्रावस्यायिनी दुःखानुबन्धिनः सुखस्य कृते सर्वथा श्रमो न वोढ़ण्यः। आयुष्ययश्च न कर्तव्यः भूतिकामेन पुरषेण। बाल्य कौमार यौवन वार्धक्याद्यवस्थासु न किंचिदपि शाश्वतसुखोपयिकं साधनमनुष्ठातुमीहते पुष्पः न्यकृतमिति विस्तृतत-त्वसारः। तथाहि बाल्यमज्ञानेन व्यतीयते। कौमारं क्रीड़ायामपसरति, यौवन च काममोहमद दर्पादिकेलेषु इन्द्रियाराम व्यवसायेषु व्यर्थं निरर्थमपयाति। अतः दैत्यबालकाः विषयवासनां परित्यज्य सर्वेन्द्रिय-प्रधनप्रेरकं नारायणं आदिदेव शरणं व्रजत। स नातिदूरे वर्तते अस्मत्तः। ह्रदि ध्विद्रवत्सतः सिद्धस्य नारायणस्य प्रीणत्म बधायाससाद्यम्। विषयातमकाः दैत्याः नारायणं पराङ्मुखीकर्वन्ति द्वेषासूयाद्यनिष्ठा-भुत्सारत चेष्टां च उपजनयन्तिं अतः विषयवासनां परित्यज्य नारायणमादिदेवं शरणं व्रजत। आसुरं भावमुन्मुच्य सर्वेषु भूतेषु कयां कुरुत। नारायणो हि सर्वेषु जनेषु पुरुषरुपेण सिथत्वा प्रेक्ष्यति। कलरूपेण सर्वत्र व्याप्तः सन्व्याप्यव्यापक भावमाप्नोति। स्वसुहृदः परमपुरूषस्य आदिदेवस्य स्वात्मार्पणमेव सकलवेदसारार्थः।[१]

To be born as a man is rare and that too it is not

1. *Ibid.* p. 165-166

permanant and hence the pleasures we derive out of sense organs have to be shunned like miseries. One should not exert one self for the sake of monetary pleasures. One should not spend one's precious life over trivial matters. Man cannot be haffy in all the four states such as childhood, boyhood, youth or old age. The childhood passes by in ignorance.

The Boyhood will be spent in playing. The young will be spent in ego and delusion. Hence one should take to Narayana. He is not far from us. Since he is within us, it is not difficult to please him. The senses in the form of demons drive us away from Narayana. Hence one should show compassion and mercy towards fellow beengs. It is Narayana who abides in everyone and instigates him to act. He is all pervasive. The crux al all the vedas is self surrender to god.

Next we have the discussion over the important topic मो I सा नविचारोपन्यास: This discussion is based on the basic point श्रीमन्मध्वमते हरि: परतर: as narrated in the ninth chapter.

The nest important topic that is dealt with under this chapter is रजतरथोत्सव and this is followed by the drama व्यासविजयम् wherein we have the nice depiction of the दशावतार

गुरुसार्वभौम सप्तरात्रीत्सवे पंचमदिनोत्सव:

Here we have the narration महारथोत्सव as an accessory of which we have the recitation सुप्रभातपद्यपञ्चक which relates itself to the life of the great saints of this philosophy;

वायोर्वत्मनि यस्य मम तस्या संप्राप्य मेधाविनः।
टीकाकृद्दर योगिवर्यगुरु राणमुख्या वितेनुर्भुवि॥
ग्रन्थान् मुक्तिपथा ऽकृहतान् सुविमलक्षानोदयान भूरिद्वाः।
तस्मै ज्ञानकलार्णवाय सततं स्यान्कृलमानंददम्॥
बादरायण सुसूत्रभावदीप प्रकाराकृदवाज धीर्गुरूः।
वेदभाष्यविवृतिं ततान याू दुर्मतानि वितथानि दइयिन्॥[1]

The grandeur रथोत्सव of the is narrated as follows;

गुरूसार्वभौमं च रथारूढ़ं विस्फारितनेत्रावलोक विस्तरैः अवलोक्यन्तः, हस्ताभ्यां साञ्जलिबन्धं प्रणमन्तः रसनेन तन्मङ्गलं नाम गृणंतः ध्राणेन तदर्पित तुलसीपुष्पपरिभक्तं धूपदीपंचाजिघ्रंतः, त्वगिन्द्रियेण तद्भगतपादान् हरिदासोत्तमाना मृदुं मन्दं स्पृशन्तः, सम्मर्दकोलाहले विना संघट्टनपीड़ां श्रोत्रेण पण्डितोत्तमैः विव्रियमाणानि कथानकानि, हरिदासैः गीयमानानि गीतानि च श्रवणगोचराणि कुर्वतः, मनसा श्री हरिगुरुमाहिमापिशुन लीलाविलासाना स्मरन्तः मननध्यानाभ्यां महत्समागमफलं तत्वनिश्लयमनुसन्दधानाः आबालवृद्धं नमो महदभ्यः नमो अर्भकेश्यः नमो युवश्यः नम आसीनेश्यः इति यथायोगं श्रीहरिविभूतीः संचिन्तयन्तः समाप्नुवन्तु जीवितसाफलयम्।[2]

Having witnessed with rept attention the Swamiji who had ascended the chariot, some of them were bowing to him, some others were reciting the noble name in their mouth, still some others were smelling the sacred Tulasi which Swamiji had offered them, the scholars in one corner were chanting Mantras, some others were remembering the prowess of Hari and pontiffs. Here the author's prowess over Rudra Sukta becomes evident as the passages नमो महदभ्यः, नमो अर्भ्रकेभ्यः is originally in the Rudra Sukta of Yajur Veda.

---

1. *Ibid.* p. 221.
2. *Ibid.* p. 222-223

Then we have been introduced to श्रीराघवेन्द्रवैभवनाटकम्

श्रीगुरुसार्वभौम सप्तरात्रोत्सवे षष्ठदिनोत्सवः

e can find a fine alliteration in the following stanza;

न मे द्या विद्या न च गुरुषु शूषुपटुता
न रिक्थं संसाराः कृनु विजयसौशील्यगुणता।
न सूक्तिः शास्त्रेषु स्वपरिहित संसाधनरतिः
तथापि त्वत्पादाम्बुज मृदु रजः प्रेरचतुर॥[१]

Nest we have been introduced to हरिदासपरिषत् under which the concepts of परम र्म and भागवत र्म have been high-lighted;

भारतदेशे भागवतधर्मः प्रत्नैराचार्यैरूपदिटः बहुधा प्रावर्तत ऋषिभिरवधूत शिखाभिरनुष्ठीयमानः। अमायया अनुवृत्या स्वविहितवृत्या भक्त्या भगवदाराधनमेव परमो धर्मः। सा ऽव भागवत धर्म इति गीयते। "धर्म प्रोज्झित कैतवोऽत्र परमो निर्मत्सराणां सतां" इति श्रीमद्भागवते प्रोज्झितकैतवत्वं परतत्वं भागवतधर्मस्य लक्षणमभिहितम्। प्रह्लाद नारद ध्रुव प्रियव्रत जनक अम्बरीशादयः भगवद्भक्ताः तमेव धर्ममनुष्ठाय सिद्धिंगताः।[१]

BHAGAVATHA DHARMA

The Bhagavatha Dharma has been preached in Bharatha by the sages and Avadhutas. The Parama Dharma is that by which a devotee prays to god frankly. The definition of Bhagavata Dharma has been given in Bhagavatha itself. Great Devotees like prahlada, Narada, Dhruva, Priyavrata, Janaka, Ambarisha and others having practiced Bhagavath Dharma have attained bliss.

---

1. *Ibid.* p. 259

DEFINITION OF SASTRA

Nest we have been introduced to the concept of Sastra according to Dvaita Vedanta here;

ऋग्यजुः सामाथर्वाण भारतं पञ्चरात्रकम्।
मूलरामायणं चैव शास्त्रमित्यभिधीयते॥[१]

The four Vedas namely Rig, Yajur, sama and Atharva, Mahabharatha, Pancharatragama and Moola Ramayana come under the purview of Sastra.

This statement has been discussed at length in the works like Vishnu Tattva Vinirnahya and others.

Next we have the discussion over Svatah Pramanya which again could be seen discussed at length in Vishnu Tatttva Vinirnaya.

Then we have Samskruta Kavi summelanam wherein the षड्ऋतुवर्णन, नदीवर्णन, पर्वतवर्णन and others remind us of some of the characteristics of Mahakavyas as mentioned in the introductory part of this essay.

श्री गुरूसार्वभौम सलरात्रोत्सवे सत्ममदिनोत्सव

The chapter begins with प्रभात गीतानि and then we have तत्वमसि वाक्यार्थ namely;

उपक्रमोपसंहारावभ्यासापूर्वताफलम्।
अर्थवादोपपत्ती च लिङ्गं तात्पर्यनिर्णये॥[१]

सर्वसमर्पणोत्सव

This is the auspicious time when the devotees offer everything to god;

श्रीगुर्वनुज्ञया अर्चकैः नीलहरितमाणिक्यमणिवज्र खचितायां कलधौतदोलायां श्री गुरूराजानां प्रतीकमादाय उत्सववृन्दावनेन साकं उपवेशितम्। ब्राह्मणाः वेद मंत्रान् पठन्तः दोचां कम्पयामासुः।

अतीव मनोज्ञोऽयं सन्निवेशः स्मर्तुं द्रष्टुं च मनोनयनयोः आप्यायमानः समभूत। समग्र सत्तरात्रोत्सवस्य साङ्गत्यसिध्यै सर्वकार्यक्लापाः श्रीगुरुसार्वभौमान्तर्गत श्रीनृहरि वेदव्यास रामचन्द्ररुपाय परमात्मने भक्त्या समर्पितः स्वगताहंभावैः श्री सुर्यमीन्द्र गुरुचरणैः सहर्षम्॥[1]

ith the instruction of the pontiff, the priests began the festivities. The photo of the revered Pontiff was placed in a cart which was studded with valuable jewels. The Brahmins touched and shook the cart with the chanting of the vedic hymns. That was a very rare sight indeed to see or to remember. This was done as part of the fitting finale to the week long celebrations which was offered to the pontiff Suyameendra Teertha finally with utmost reverence.

This is being followed by the speech of the pontiff which portrayed the highest Dharmic and Philosophical ideals in a simple straight forward language.

पंचमुखी प्राणदेवसंदर्शनं-चम्पूसमर्पणं च

Here we have the relevance of the prefix pancha-mukhi of the author;

गुरुराजानां उपासनापीठः रायरगाद्दिगे इति प्रसिद्धं दरीदृश्यते तत्रैवास्मत्प्रपितामहाः यरगेरि पण्डित वेंकटाचार्याः, द्वादशाब्दं तपः कृत्वा श्रीहरिवायुगुरुप्रसादं प्राऽतवन्तः। अतऽव तेषां पंचमुखहनूमद्-भजकः इति गृहनाम रूढं भूत्वा तद्वंशास्य पंचमुखीत्युपनाम प्रचलितं व्यवहारेषु। तद्वंशजोऽहम।[2]

The Upasana Peetha of the revered Gurus is known as rayara Gaddige. There my great grand father by name Yarageri Pandita Venkatacharya had the grace of Harivayus after performing penance for twelve Years.

1. *Ibid.* p. 302
2. *Ibid.* p. 310

Hence from that day onwards they got the prefix panchamukhi attached to their name as they had the grace of panchamukha Hanuman. I belong to their illustrious family.

चम्पूसमर्पणं

As I was instructed by the revered Suyameendra Teertha so am I offering this champu work at his feet;

श्रीगुरूराघवेन्द्र पदपंकज दत्तचित्रः श्रीसुययमीन्द्रमुनिभिः चम्पूप्रबन्ध-निर्माणे नियुक्तो गुर्वाज्ञां पूरयित्वा यथाविभवे तं समर्पचितुम-भिलषाभि।[1]

The author completes this monumental work with the following

फलश्रुतिः

यो भकत्या गुरूराघवेन्द्रचरणद्वन्द्व स्मरन्यः पठेत
स्तोत्रं दिव्यमिदं सदा नहि भवेत्तस्यामुखं किंचन।
किंत्विष्टार्थसमृद्दिरेव कमलानाथप्रसादोपयात्
कीर्तिर्दिग्विदिता विभूतिरतुला साक्षी दध्यास्योऽत्रहि॥[2]

One who reads this champu devotedly by remembering the sacred feet of Sri Guru Raghavendra will never come across any impediments in life, but on the contrary their aims and aspirations will be fulfilled.

Thus this champu has beautiful Alanharas, charming descriptions,highest philosophical tenets and grand intellectual debates all combined into one. The descriptions are very realistic as the author has written this with has personal experience and it is not a myth or a legend which would be far from reality. The mastery of the poet over the Sanskrit Language as well as Kannada at times is something astounding and he hs certainly derived the grace of the god for the composition of this work.

1. Ibid. p. 310
2. Ibid. p. 314

5

VIDYAVACASPATI SHAMBHULINGESWARA VIJAYA CHAMPU

PANDARINATHACHARYA GALAGALI -1982

Shambhulingeswara Vijaya Champu a Champu work written by Pandit Padarinathacharya Galagali was published in the year 1982 from Brihanmatha, Bijapur which is a biography of Sri Shambhulingeswara a great contemporary scholar and saint. The work has great historical value as it dipicts rivers, mountains, holy places pertaining to Karnataka in particular and India in general.

INCENTIVE

The author Galagali has in brief mentioned in his introduction regarding the incentive for the work , the purpose of the work, etc. The incentive for the work is that some of the followers of the tradition of Brihanmutt requested him to compose a work in Sanskrit in Champu style depicting the life of Shambhulinga on par with Kadambari, Dashakumara

Charita and champu Bharatha and secondly the author had also reverence regarding the Shambhulinga. This made him to write the work;

कतिपयकालानन्तरं केचन श्रीशिवाचार्यचम्पूभक्ताः मदन्तिक-मुपगत्य स्वगुरुणा चारूचरितं संस्कृतभाषायां श्रीमद्धि रूपेण गुम्फनीयं चम्पूरिति व्यजिज्ञपन् कादम्बरी दशकुमारचरित चम्पूभारतादि प्रागलभ्य-सरण्यामिति, ममापि मनसि आसीदेव श्रीशिवयोगिनां विषये निरतिशय आदरः।[1]

STAND POINT OF THE POET.

The poet also makes his stand clear in his introduction that this is a historical account of the life and greatness of the Sivayogi and the hero is the Shambhulinga himself. The work depicts the greatness and supremacy of Virasaivism and has no Dvaita leaning and the poet says that he is only a scribe who has depicted the thoughts regarding the saint heard directly from the saint or by his disciples in Kannada and he has just translated it into Sanskrit and his job is only that of a translator and not anything more than that;

अयं च चम्पूप्रबन्धः श्रीशिवायार्चाणां चरित्रात्मकः। अस्य खलु महाप्रबन्धस्य खलु स ङव नायकः। अस्मिन्समग्रेऽपि ग्रन्थे तेषामेव मतस्य, धर्मस्य, श्रद्धायाः सम्प्रदायास्य, आचारस्य च श्रेष्ठत्वं उत्तमत्वं प्राच्य प्राधान्यं च तदाज्ञानुसारेण प्रतिपादितमस्ति। नेदं माध्व वध्व वन्यध्व वनीनसय मम मतं सम्मतं वा। अहं तु केवलं अत्र लिपिकारः। तैर्वा तद्भक्तैर्वा यद् कन्नड़भाषायां लिखितं सूचितं वा तत संस्कृतभाषाया केवलं मया विपरिवर्तितम्। ईदृशेषु मतीयविषयेषु मम पात्रं केवलं भाषान्तरकारस्यैव॥[2]

---

1. Sri Shambhulinga Vijaya Champu-Pandarinathacharya Galagali, Brihanmutt, Bijapur-1982, p. xxxvii.
2. *Ibid.* p. xli

PURPOSE OF THE WORK

The poet also clarifies the purpose of the work that he has written it to acquire fame and to know the ways of the world; परं मयातु शिवाचार्यगुणलुब्धेन केवलं यशसे पर निर्वृतये च निबद्धोयं प्रबन्धः।।[1]

The poet has written thirty three stanzas before the commencement of the work with which one can note his प्रतिज्ञा and about his hero;

प्रतिज्ञा

He takes an oath while he is commencing his work;

नामं नामं गुरूस्तोमं कामं क्षेमकरं हरम्।
शम्भुलिङ्गशिवाचार्य वृत्तचम्पू समारभे।।[2]

विनय

The modesty of the poet is revealed in some of the following stanzas;

क्व क्लिष्टा संस्कृतं भाषा क्व चम्पूः शिलष्टबन्धुरा।
क्व चाहं जड़धीर्मन्दः जाड्यादेवोपपध्यते।।[3]

Where is that difficult Sanskrit Language and where is Champu an abstruse style? where am I a dullard ? This stanza resembles the second stanza of the first canto of Raghuvamsha;

क्व सूर्यप्रभवो वंशः क्वचाल्प विषयामतिः।
तितीर्षुः दुस्तरं मोहात् उडुपेनास्मि सागरम्।।

Further the poet says modestly;

अणुर्वापि कणोवात्र गुणश्चेत्सा गुरोः कृपा।
दोषाः शेषां ममाज्ञत्वविशेषा इति भाव्यताम्।।[4]

---

1. *Ibid.* p. xli
2. *Ibid.* p. 4
3. *Ibid.* p. 6
4. *Ibid.* p. 7

If there is an element of merit in my work it is due to the grace of the guru and if there are any mistake it is due to my faulty composition.

The justification of the hero is nicely brought out here;

शम्भुलिङ्गशिवाचार्यो ज्ञानमेरूर्महागुरूः।
जङ्गमज्ञानकोशोऽयं भाति विध्यास्वयंवर॥[1]

Shambhulinga Shivacharya is an embodiment of knowledge like Mount Meru and he is a walking encyclopedia who is wedded to knowledge.

There are nine Tarangas or divisions in this work and in the first Taranga we get a historical glimpse of the glory of Karnataka, the great scholar, saints of Karnataka like Sankara, Ramanuja and Madhwa the religious tolerance of the Vijayanagar kings, the history of Brihan Matha, Hyder's invasion and so on. An attempt has been made here to highlight some of the above mentioned points to evaluate the style of the poet;

KARNATAKA

तस्याश्च कर्मभूमिरिति प्रथिमानं धर्मभूमिरिति महिमान
मनुपमानमेव सम्मानं च समासादितवत्या भगवत्या
भारतक्षित्या अत्युज्वलकर्णाकुण्डल मुण्डनतामुपयाति
अखण्डमिदं कर्णटक महीमण्डलं यद्वैभवसमुपवर्णने
चक्षुष्कर्णकुल चक्रवर्त्यपि न प्रभुः प्रतिभाति।[2]

In the following passages we find mention to the artistic supremacy of Karnataka;

हलेबीडु हम्पी ऽहोले पट्टदक्ल्लु गदग लक्कुड़ि मैसूरू बेलूरू

1. *Ibid.* p. 5
2. *Ibid.* p. 12

प्रभृति पट्टणग्रामेषु कर्णाटकप्रान्तीयैः वास्तुविध्याविदग्धैः मूर्तिशिल्प-कलाकुशलैः स्थापतिभिः चित्रकारैः तक्षकैश्च निर्मितानि सूक्ष्माति-सूक्ष्माणि महामहन्ति च प्रस्तरखण्डविस्तारित वास्तुशिल्पानि, बृहच्छैलखण्डस्य अखण्डैकगण्ड शिलायामुत्कीर्णाः कौशल्यप्रतिमाः, दिव्यभव्या गृहाः। अतिसुन्दराणि देवमन्दिराणि, सौन्दर्येण अप्रतिमाः प्रतिमाः, स्फुटच्चैतन्य स्फूर्तय इव देवतामूर्तयः आश्चर्यस्तंभित प्रेक्षक कदम्बाः, स्पर्शनक्षण ञव समुदञ्चतसजस्वरारथ्याः संचुम्बितसरपर पुरांध्रिकापादानुपूर गोपुराः चित्रविचित्राणि शैलशिलोंदृकितानि दक्षिणोत्तरशिल्पशैली कौशलीसमुन्मिलित चंचत्पात्रालिका विविध भावभङ्गी हृदयंगम द्दश्यचित्राणि....रोमांचयति शिल्पशास्त्रविलक्षणात् उन्नमयति च कर्णाटिकमातुः प्रतिष्ठाशिरः किरीटम्॥[1]

Shankara

The greatness and the achievements of Shankara are depicted effectively here;

त ञते पाखण्डादिचण्ड दुर्मतषण्ड खण्डनपण्डिता मण्डनमिश्रादि मीमांसा पण्डितवेतण्ड मण्डलमत गण्डभेदेन प्रचण्डपुण्डरीकः मुण्डिकलाखण्डलः वैदिक जन हृत्प्रण्डरीक विकासकचण्ड मयूरवायमानाः श्रीमच्छ्रीशंकरभगवत्पादाः केरलदेशधृतजन्मनोऽपि कर्णटकदेशस्य महतीं निद्याय अत्रत्यामेव तुङ्गतुङ्गोतरङ्ग संघात संघतिस्संघां श्टङ्गेरी स्वतपोभूमिं कार्यक्षेत्रं च विधाय महांसस्थासानं च संस्थाप्य इत ञव सर्वसर्वसहायां स्वाद्वैतमतं प्रसारयामासुः।[2]

RAMANUJA

Ramanuja's contribution is narrated nicely here;

तथैव च श्रीमद्रामचरणाव्ज षट्चरणाः सदाचरण शास्तप्रचारण देवपादपरिचरण परायणाः श्री रामानुजाख्या शिष्टविशिष्टपण्डितश्रेष्ठ

---

1. *Ibid.* p. 15
2. *Ibid.* p. 15

समभिष्ठुताः सर्वजातिजनाङ्ग समुद्धारबद्धादराः विशिष्टाद्वैतमत संप्रदाय पर्वतकालार्यपादाः देशान्तरगृहीत जनुषोऽपि कर्णटकमातुः हृदयस्थानायमानं क्षेत्रमुपगत्य चिरतरमध्युष्य राजानायमधिगत्य जनानुरागमासाध्य च श्रीवैष्णवसिद्धान्तं भारतभुवः कोणे कोणे प्रसारयामासुः।[1]

MADHWACHARYA

Madhwas contribution to Indian philosophy is picturesquely portrayed here;

तथैव श्री मध्वमुनिनामानः भेदसिद्धान्तप्रसारण बद्धादराः विदृद्धोरेयाः सुप्रसिद्धा सिद्धपुरुषाः परशुरामक्षेत्रमिति प्रथिमानमुपागते कर्णटकभूमातुः कर्णकुण्डलायमाने उडपीमण्डले मध्यगेहनामक गृहस्थ लब्धजन्मा न सर्वत्रापि प्रसारयामासुः द्वैतदर्शनम्॥[2]

Religious tolerance of Vijayanagar

Religious tolerance of Vijayanagar kings is vividly brought out here;

तपोगरिष्ठैर्महिममहिष्ठैः श्रीविध्यारण्यमहास्वामिभिः वीरवरेण्य दीनशरण्य हक्कबुक्केति नवरसहकारेण पम्पापति परमानुग्रह भूम्ना च तुङ्गातरङ्गिणी तुङ्गतरसंघटि गणरङ्गस्थलायमाने हम्पीक्षेत्रे सुप्रतिष्ठिते कर्णाटकसाम्राज्ये बुक्कराजादारभ्य श्रीकृष्णदेवरायपर्यन्तं...वात्सल्यशश्च मूर्तयः औदार्यशेवधयः प्रजारंजनैकव्रताः सर्वधर्मप्रोत्साहकाः सकलभाषापोषकाः समस्तजातिमताचार पुरस्कार कारका...अत ऽव तस्मिन्विजयनगरे शैव, वीरशैव, वैष्णव, शाक्त, कापालिक, तांत्रिक, मीमांसक नैयायिकादि विविध जातिमतपथाचार संप्रदाय प्रवर्तकाचायणिां मठपीठादिप्रतिष्ठा प्रारभ्य ऽवावर्तिष्ठ राजाश्रयप्रोत्साह परिकर्मिताः॥[3]

---

1. *Ibid.* p. 15
2. *Ibid.* p. 16
3. *Ibid.* p. 20

THE HISTORY OF THE BRIHANMUTT

One can note the free flowing style of the poet here;

शैवपीठेषु प्रकृष्टं वीरशैवपीठेषु प्रधानं, श्रीरेणुक सम्प्रदायमठेषु महत्तरं गणधीशसंस्थानेषु मुख्यतमं च तं बहन्मठपीठमारूढ़ेषु विद्वद्राजिशिरोराजि कटकुण्डल राजि नीराचितचरण राजीवानां साक्षाद्विरूपाक्ष करूणा कटाक्षाभि लक्षित रक्षितानां...अनन्यसामान्याः श्रीबृहन्मठाधीश्वराः बहव एव विश्वविध्याविभूतिपुरुषाः संबभूवुः॥[1]

HYDER'S INVASION

Hyder's invasion and the birth of the hero of the work is portrayed here;

एवं चक्रनेमिक्रमेण कालचक्रभूमिभाग्यमाणेषु पाणिषु, संसरति संसारे, व्यतीतेषु वत्सरेषु, गच्छति च महीयसि अनेहसि यवनराजपुरुषः हैदरालिः केलदीसंस्थानमाचक्रम महता बलेन...तेषामेव वंशकेतु भूतस्य द्वितीय श्रीसिद्धेश्वरशास्त्रि महोदयस्य सत्पुत्रः श्रीसदाशिवनामा ब्रह्मतेजस्वी मुनिमहर्षि वर्चस्वी महामनस्वी लोकोत्तरतपस्वी समाजार्चित सर्वस्वी अध्यात्मपथक्रमण तरस्वी मिहिरमहस्वी ज्ञानविज्ञान वैदग्ध्योजस्विी सत्पुरुषो महापरुष एव एतच्चम्पू प्रबन्धस्य प्रधाननायकः॥[2]

In this Taranga we have the descriptions of Brihanmatt tradition, Siddheswara Pandita, Channamamba, the birth of Sadasiva, his intelligence and so on.

BRIHANMUTT TRADITION

The tradition of the Mutt was to do अन्नदान to the students irrespective of their Gotras and Sri Siddheswara Pandita the father of Sadasiva inherited this tradition;

---

1. *Ibid.* p. 21
2. *Ibid.* p. 26

अन्नदानं च छात्राणां यत्राहोरात्रमप्यहो।
प्रचालयतीति क्षुत्क्षामकुक्षीणां तृप्तये मुदे॥
छात्राणं सर्वगोत्राणामन्नछात्रायितो मठः।
ज्ञानसत्रस्यसुक्षेत्रं शिवेक्षापात्रतामगात्॥
ऽतत्परम्पराप्राप्ते बृहन्मठपथानुगे
वंशे महेश्वरे जातः श्रीसिद्धेश्वर पण्डितः॥[१]

THE GREATNESS OF SIDDHESWARA PANDITA

The greatness of Siddheswara Pandita who had superior intellect, whose mind was soft, who had expertise in knowledge, who was handsome to look at who was an adept in the daily ways of life, who was highly regarded in the society and whose fame spread far and wide is nicely presented here;

सोऽयं सिद्धेश्वरपण्डितः सुनिमील निगमागमाध्ययन सिद्धप्रचण्ड पाण्डितीमण्डितः यथार्थ्यमुपलम्भयामास स्वकीयं शुभनाम। क्रमेण च वयसि प्रौढ़िमानं, मनसि कोमलिमानं, विध्यायां गरिमाणं, स्वभावे मृदुमानं वपुषि प्रथिमानं, व्यवहारे चतुरिमाणं समाजे च बहुमानं समुपेयुष सिद्धेश्वरपण्डितस्य सर्वत्र प्रससार शारदाशर्वरीशर्वरी सार्वभौम ज्योत्सनाजाल धवलं सुनिर्मलं यशः॥[२]

He had a wife by name Channamamba who was a match to his beauty, to his qualities, a lady with spotless character, who was like his shadow who hailed from the city of Haveri with Harasur Brihanmutt tradition;

तस्य रूपानुरूपा गुणानुगुणा शीलानुकूला स्वभावानुवर्तिनी

1. *Ibid. p.* 18
2. *Ibid. p.* 18

छायोपजीविनी पदानुगामिनी संचरन्तीव सौदामिनी हावेरी पत्तनस्य समूह बृहन्मठीयानां वंशसमुत्पन्ना चन्नमाम्बा नाम्नी कन्यामणि जग्राह पाणिं शास्त्रोक्त विधिना विधिनानुप्रेरिता।[१]

She gave birth to a son on शालीवाहनशक १८०९ विश्वजित्संवत्सर, माघशुद्धदशमी बुधवासर मृगशिरानक्षत्रे and in the year 1888.

समुपपध्यत तेजः प्रकर्षतुलितकुमारः चिदानन्दस्वरूप स्मारित-सनत्कुमारः जन्मप्रभृति जितमारः कश्चन सुकुमारः कुमारः शालीवाहन-शकाब्दे १८०९ मिते वर्षे विश्वजिसंवत्सरस्य माघशुद्धदशम्यां बुधवासरे मृगशिरा नक्षत्रयुक्ते ऽेन्द्रप्रयोगे इसवीये १८८८ तमे वत्सरे।[२]

As the boy was born on account of the God Siva he was named as Sadasiva;

शुभे शोभने च सुमुहूर्ते सदाशिवपरमानुग्रह समुद्भवस्य स्वस्य सुतस्य सदाशिव इत्येव चकार नाम नामकरणप्रसङ्गे सम्मिलित सकलबन्धु मित्रदायादिसंघे पिता सिद्धेश्वरः।।[३]

At the age of two, the boy got the teeth and with that the teethache and gradually the boy became blind;

यदासौ सदाशिवबालः द्वितीये वर्षे पदमर्पयत, दन्तकङ्कलांकरोद्गमः समलक्ष्यत। कतिपयैरेव मासैः दंतपंक्त्याविभवि पीड़ितोऽसौ बालकः महतीमेवान्वभूध्यातनाम्। क्रमेण च उल्बणतामुपेतया अन्ध डाव संवृत्तः सुकुमारः स कुमारः।।[४]

But the parents with their attitudes of treating the guests, by giving food, by helping others and respecting the elders restored back the sight to Sadasiva;

1. *Ibid. p.* 18
2. *Ibid. p.* 19
3. *Ibid. p.* 20
4. *Ibid. p.* 21

तथ्येन पथ्येन तस्या अतिशयेन, हरगुरु समाराधनेन अन्नदानेन, परेपकरणेन, महनीय साधुपरितोषेन, कतिपयेष्वेव दिवसेषु नयन पाटवमधिजगाम सदाशिवः, त्रिलोचनानुग्रहभूम्ना अल्पीयस्येव काले विलोचनः कुमारः समजनि सलोचनः सदालीचनश्च॥[1]

The firm resolve and attitude of Sadasiva to life is nicely portrayed here;

धनाशोदक्षिणाशा वा नास्त्येव मम सर्वथा।
धनं हि निधनं मन्ये प्रधानं ज्ञानमेव मे॥
ब्रह्मविध्यैव विध्योक्ता सा विध्या या विमुक्तये।
शतायुर्वा गतायुर्वा साधये तां प्रयत्नतः॥
श्रीरेणुकांघ्रिप्ररेणूनां त्रसरेणुर्भवाम्यहम्।
चतुः पुत्रेषु मामेकं रेणाकार्याय यच्छत॥[2]

I do not have desire to earn money and in fact I consider money as death and knowledge is the main thing. Whether I live for hundred years or die soon I am going to learn Brahma Vidya by learning which I will be eligible for salvation. I will be at the feet of Renuka and please spare me for this cause as you have four children.

तृतीयस्तरङ्ग

Sadasiva leaving the house for देशाटन wherein he comes across Bangalore, Srirangapatna, Mysore, he acquiring mastery over various Sastras, visiting Kashi, participating in intellectual debates and defeating them, studying higher branches of learning like Logic, Grammar, Vedanta, Mimamsa under great acharyas is effectively portrayed here;

---

1. *Ibid.* p. 34
2. *Ibid.* p. 39

BANGALORE

The Bangalore with its multifaced splendor as seen by Sadasiva is as follows;

यत्खलु नगरं व्यापारकेन्द्रमिति वैश्यैः वीरस्थानमिति क्षत्रियैः, ब्रह्मपुरीति ब्राह्मणैः, उपतीवनाधार इति शूद्रैः, सिद्धायतनमिति साधकैः, मल्लशालेति मल्लैः, सङ्गीतरङ्गभूमिरिति गायकैः, कलानिकेतनमिति वादकैः, नृत्यमण्डपमिति नर्तकैः, राजकीय सूत्रचालन केन्द्रमिति शासकैः, कल्पवृक्षमिति भिक्षुकैः, संकेतस्थानमिति वेश्याभिः, शारदापीठ इति पण्डितैः, अदृष्टद्वारमिति वृत्तिकामुकैः, यंत्रनगरमिति विज्ञानिभिः मुक्तिमन्दिरमिति सन्यासिभिः, लाभ क्षेत्रमिति व्ययसायिभिः। न्यायालय इति वादिभिः, विज्ञानभवनमिति स्थपतिभिः सौख्यस्थानमिति निश्चिन्त-गृहस्थैः आश्रितं च शोभते।[1]

This city is viewed as a business centre by businessmen, the warrior class consider it to be a royal ground,the Brahmins consider it to be a Brahmapuri, the Sudras consider it as a place of livelihood, for those who are Sadhakas it is like a Siddhayatana, for the wrestlers it is a place of wrestling, it is a music hall for the musicians, for Politicians it is a political centre, for beggars it is a Kalpavruksha, for prostitutes it is a meeting place, for scholars it is an abode of learning, for job seekers it is an open door, for scientists it is a city of science, for mendicants it is a place for salvation, for the farmers it is a place to make profits, for lawyers it is a place of courts and for the householders it is a safe place to live.

SRIRANGAPATNA

Next , Sadasiva saw Srirangapatna;

---

1. *Ibid.* p. 46

तत्र च मङ्गलकावेरी तरङ्गिणी प्लवङ्गमुङ्गीत्तङ्ग तरङ्गान्तरङ्ग रङ्गीतसंगोच्छलद्वीती माला दोला लीला लोलाविल बालोत्तेलतावकीर्ण सलिलशीकरनिकर कीरवित तारकित सैकत तीरं, चिरदूर परिभ्रमण परिखिन्न सूर्य स्पन्दन तुरग तृषापनोदनाय कावेरीजलं स्वफल कमण्ड़लेष्वादाय जलदानोध्यतैरिव गगनाङ्गण सार्वभौमेरिव नभोयात्रोध्यत सप्तर्षिमण्डल स्वागताय पूर्णकुम्भ साहित्यसन्नद्ध भूलोक प्रतिनिधिभिरिव, भूप्रदक्षिणोध्युक्त सूर्याचन्द्रमसोः गौरवाय चामरसेवामित तन्वानैः अपरिमित नारिकेल पादपैः परिवृतं, कवेरकन्या तटिनी तटस्थलनिर्मापितं, गगनचुम्बिगोपुरशिखर प्राकार परिशोभयानं सुन्दरतर श्रीरङ्गनाथस्वामि देवालयसनाथं विशाल शालि वनशालि नाना प्रेक्षणीयस्थान लक्षणीयं, अनेकैतिहासिक वस्तु विस्तारैः विश्व विस्मापकं, भूतकाल संवृत्तनैक निर्णायक घटनास्मारकं हिन्दूयवनोभय जातीय जनानां पवित्र क्षेत्रायमाणं यवनराजपुरुषेण टिप्पूसुल्ताननाम्ना पश्चिमवाहिनीकावेरी नीरस्य दक्षिणदेशगसुप्रसिद्ध श्रीरङ्ग नामक महाक्षेत्र प्रतिस्पर्धितया महता प्रयत्नेन महादेव निर्मापितं दुर्निरूप्य तत्सौस्स्त्य सारूप्य संप्राप्य साद्रूप्य प्रशस्यं कावेर्याः पश्चिमवादिप्रवाह यात्रायमाण परिसरप्रतिष्ठत निसर्गसौन्दर्य निकेतनं श्रीरङ्गपट्टणं चक्षुषो लक्षीलकार।[१]

Sri Rangapatna is beautiful on account of the revered Kaveri river whose waves create ripples and which appear as though it is inviting the seven seas to take bath in it. Very nearby there is an old Ranganatha Temple which has a lofty tower and a beautiful architecture, a place which makes people remember about many ancient spots pertaining to Hindus and Muslims wherein the historically famous Tippu ruled and the place has scenic beauty as the whole area is surrounded by many coconut trees.

MYSORE

Next, Sadasiva perceived Mysore the historically famous city in all its splendor;

1. *Ibid.* p. 48-49

संध्याकाले दूरादेव अदृश्यत बालचन्द्र जालायमान सहस्रसहस्र विध्युद्दीप माला दूरीकृत नैश तिमिर स्तोमव्यापारं इतस्तनः चेतनोचित चंचला ययवत संचलञ्चल चंचलाक्षीसंचार चुंचरं चतुष्पथचत्वर केन्द्रस्थानास्थापित राजप्रमुखप्रतिमा परिसरोपवन मध्यजल कुण्डोच्छ-लत्सलिल नलिका मुखोद्गीर्यमाणेदक धारासार सीकरनिरन्तराविभ-विदिन्द्रलाप सौन्दर्य मनोहरं समासादित लक्ष्मीप्रसाद सूचक प्रासाद पंक्ति परिशोभमानं चतुरमति वणिक्प्रवर चाणक्य तंत्र बन्दीभूत चंचललक्ष्मीनिरन्तर नवनाद्ध निकेतनायमान मुक्तारत्नराजि विराजि विपणि वीथि विराजिने नैक संस्कृत वेदपाठशाला भवनायिन्द श्रूयमाण छात्रवृन्द गीयमान मंजुल वेदघोषध्वनि पावित परिसरं पथिमिलत्शाला कलाशला विध्यार्थि विध्यार्थिनी दल चर्च्यमाण विज्ञानेतिहास गणितभाषा शास्त्रादि विषयैः। अनाच्छादित वीथी विश्वविध्यालय संपन्नमिव लक्ष्यमाणं, तत्र तत्र परिदृश्यमान नानादेवालयद्वार वातायन रंध्राद्गच्छदगुरु गुग्गुलु धूपगन्ध सन्तर्पित पण्यवीथी संचारिजनं धार्मिक-कार्मिक। दीन-धनिक, पण्डित-पामर, स्त्री-पुरुष, विध्यार्थि-विध्यार्थिनी, नास्तिक-आस्तिकादि विविध वर्ग जाति जन जनाङ्ग संकीर्णं महीशूरनामकं नगरम्।[1]

In the evenings one can witness the thousands of lights which dispel darkness, the broad roads, the veda ghosha which is echoing everywhere, the students who are perceiving knowledge in various branches of learning pertaining to science, history etc in the Universities, the sacred smoke of the Arathi of the deities emanating from the temples, different class of people like religious, working class poor and the rich, heterodox and the orthodox people living together.

---

1. *Ibid.* p. 50-51

STUDY OF SADASIVA

Sadasiva studied Mahakavyas , Khandakavyas, Gadyakavyas, texts pertaining to Alankara sastra, Basic grammar , Music and others;

STUDY OF MAHAKAVYAS

माघस्य अमोघकृतिं शिशुपालवधं आचूलमूलमभ्यस्य संस्कृत-साहित्य सरसिजाकार विकासक भारवेः काव्ये अर्थगौरवं शब्दमाधुर्यं, भाव गाम्भीर्यं, सरसभाषणचातुर्यं, राजनीति चातुर्यं च दृष्ट्वा, नैषधं विद्वदौषधमिति पृथ्वीप्रथितं नैषधीयचरितं नाम महामहत्तरं श्रीहर्षस्य काव्यमधीतवान्।[1]

Having studied Magha's Sisupalavadha in detail, having observed the subtleity of meaning, the crispness of the dialogues and the political acumen in Bharavi's Kiratarjuniya he studied Sri Harsha's Naishadhiya charita which is known as a brain tonic even to the scholars;

KHANDAKAVYAS AND GADYAKAVYAS

वासवदत्ता, कादम्बरी हर्षचरित, दशकुमारचरितादीनि गद्य-काव्यानि, मेघदूत, सूर्यदूत सूर्यशतक, सौन्दर्यलहरी, गीतगोविन्द, भामिनीविलास, गाथासप्तशती, गङ्गालहरी, सुभाषितसाहस्री, पादुका-सहस्रादि सहस्राधिक खण्डकाव्यानि अपि गुरूनिरपेक्षमेव स्वयं समुत्पन्न काव्यव्युत्पत्तिबलेन अनुवाचितवान्॥[2]

Without a teacher with his own abilities, Sadasiva mastered prose works like Vasavadatta, Kadambari, Harsha Charita, Dashakumara Charita, Lyrics like Meghaduta, Surya Shataka, Soundarya Lahari, Gita Govinda, Bhamini Vilasa, Gatha Sapthashati, Gangala-

1. *Ibid.* p. 54
2. *Ibid.* p. 55

hari, Subhashita Sahasri, Paduka Sahasra and other texts.

TEXTS PERTAINING TO ALANKARA SASTRA

Sadasiva studied some of the basic texts pertaining to Alankara Sastra such as Kuvalayanada, Sahitya Darpana, Kavya Prakasha, Dhvanyaloka, Rasa Gangadhara, Kavyadarsha and others;

नन्दं कुवलयानन्दमनुाच्चान्वविन्दत
साहित्यदर्पणे तस्य साहित्यस्यान्तरात्मनः
काव्यप्रकाशे हृदयावकाशे ज्ञानप्रकाशं किरतीह तस्य
ध्वन्यहवन्यधनीनस्य बभूवानन्दवर्धन
रसगङ्गाधरे तस्य रसगङ्गोगमागमाः
काव्यादर्शे ददर्शायं विश्वरूपं विविच्य च।[1]

BASIC GRAMMAR

Sadasiva mastered Laghu Siddhanta Kaumudi and Astadhyayi within a short span of time;

लघुसिद्धान्तकौमुध्या अलघु ज्ञानमाप सः।
वैयाकरणभाण्डार कवाटोद्घाटकुञ्चिकाम्॥[2]

MUSIC

Sadasiva mastered his knowledge in Music under the guidance of Veene Seshanna;

परेध्युः प्रातः काल ए़व तपा मैसूरूमण्डल ए़व सङ्गीत गङ्गाधर इति प्रख्यातिं समीयुषां वैणिक शिखामणि शेषण्ण महोदयानां पट्टशिष्यत्व सौभाग्य याजनीभूतानां गानयोगि श्री पष्ठहस्वामिनां सविधमुपसृत्य स्वकीयां सङ्गीतशिक्षणाकांक्षामाचचक्षे।[3]

1. *Ibid.* p. 56
2. *Ibid.* p. 57
3. *Ibid.* p. 57

VISIT TO KASHI

Sadasiva made up his mind to visit Kashi as he wanted to master various Sastras. Here is a pen picture of Kashi:

कैलासपति करूणा कल्लोलिनी जलक्षालितं अनेकानेक देवताधिष्ठितं सहस्रादिकदेवमन्दिर देदीप्यमानं, परमेश्वर नित्यसन्निधानमहितं अविमुक्तक्षेत्रमिति जगत्प्रसिद्धिमाप्तं, प्रतिवीथी विध्योतमान वेदशास्त्र पाठशाला श्रूयमाण वेदघोष दूरीकृत पातकपटलं प्रतिगृह प्रवर्तमान शास्त्रीय वाक्यार्थ कलकल मुखर दिञ्मुखं दूरदूरदेश समागत यात्रिकैः गङ्गास्नान समयोच्चार्यमाण "हरहर महादेव गङ्गाधर गौरीपते" इति शिव शुभनाम ध्वनिध्वस्त समस्त दुरितं नित्यसौवास्ति कृन्कृत्तिवास शिखण्डमण्डन खण्डेन्द्रजोस्ना जाल प्रनस्कतीकृत सुधालेप धवल धाम स्तोमाभिरामं महोदण्ड; पण्डित पुण्डरीक खण्डमान प्रचण्ड पाखण्डमतं प्रध्वस्त समास्त नास्तिक्यं, आश्रयं श्रुतीनां, आधारं स्मृतीनां परिष्कार पुरोष्ठ पुराणानां, संस्करणसदनं संस्काराणं, शोधनभूमिः संप्रदायानां, संरक्षणगृहं सनातन धर्मस्य विहारभूमिं मुक्तिसीमन्तिन्याः, विश्रान्तिवेदिं शान्तिदेवतायाः संजीवनीशैले कलिकवलितास्तिक्यस्य। कायकल्पकेन्द्र वीरशैव संप्रदायस्य मृत्युसोपानं कलेः रुद्रभूमिं निरीश्वर वादस्य, पुत्यदेशं भौतविलासस्य, सुभदकोटिं वैदिकमतस्य, स्वयं व्यक्तिस्थलीं दैविकशक्तेः, अवतारभुवः विभूतिरूपाणां, प्रत्यक्षगोचर-स्थानं मंत्रसिद्धानां, संक्षिप्तावृत्तिं कैलासस्य, प्रनरुक्तिं सत्यलोकस्य, विस्तरणं श्वेतद्वीपस्य, उपनगरं वैकुण्ठस्य, प्रतिद्वन्द्वपत्तनं अमरावत्याः, बीजनिष्पादन क्षेत्रं ज्ञानसंस्थानां, निक्षेपस्थानं अध्यात्मसंपत्तेः, शिल्पगृहं पाण्डित्यप्रतीकानां, अज्ञान पण्डित वेतण्डानां, गारूड़नीड़ं सौगतसरी-सृपाणां सिंहगृहं स्याद्वादमत्तमातङ्गानां, विहारवनं तार्किककेसरिणां, अभयारण्यं वैयाकरणशार्दूलानां, सुवर्णपञ्चरं मुक्तिहंसस्य, सत्वापूरण-विधिं तत्वज्ञानस्य, श्रुतिविवृतं, स्मृतिसंस्तुतं, पुराणप्रसिद्धम्, आगमानु-वर्णितं, इतिहासप्रथितं, मुक्तिक्षेत्रं, क्षेत्रराजं परमपुमर्थदतीर्थ सार्थसार्वभौम काशीपत्तनं उपासीदत सदाशिवः।[1]

1. *Ibid.* p. 60

Sadasiva came to Kashi which is sanctified on account of Ganga, wherein innumerable temples are erected for gods, wherein every street has Veda pathashalas, wherein the chanting of vedas are reverberating, where in the intellectual debates on various Sastras could be perceived, where in one can listen to Hara hara Maḥadev, Gangadhara Gowripathe slogan emanating from the mouths of pilgrims who have come there from far off places, where in the heterodox systems of philosophy have been criticised everyday, which is the abode of the Vedas, which is the substratum for all smritis, where in all the puranas will be modified, which is the abode of the samskaras, where in the Sampradaya is strictly followed, which is the abode of all the peace loving gods, which is the place where Veerasaivism got popularised, which is the crematorium for all the heterodox systems of philosophy, which is the concise form of Kailasa, which is the repetition of Satyaloka, which is an extension of Svetadweepa, which is a short form of Vaikunta, which is like Garuda to the Buddhist snakes, which is like a lion to the jaina intoxicated elephants, which is a pleasure garden to the Logicians, which is like a sanctuary to the tigers in the form of Grammarians, which is like a golden cage to those who aspire for salvation, which is famous in Sruti, Smriti, puranas, Agamas, Itihasas and the greatest of the holy places.

STUDY OF VARIOUS SASTRAS IN KASHI

Sadasiva studied तर्कसंग्रह, दीपिका, मुक्तावली, प्रभा, दिनकरी, मंजूषा, पंचलक्षणी, गादाधरी, चतुर्दशलक्षणी, सिद्धन्त लक्षणी, पक्षता, शतकोटि, सत्प्रतिपक्ष, सामान्यनिरुक्त, व्युत्पत्तिवाद and शक्तिवाद under Logic;

तर्कसंग्रहनामानमग्ट्टेभहेन कृतां कृतिम् दीपिकातर्कसुज्ञात प्राणिका प्रापि तद्दिया मुक्तावल्यापायत्लभारतं व्युत्पत्तिकुसुमं सता प्रभा दिनकरीव्याख्ये मुख्ये मुक्तावली कृतेत्वा तर्कप्रमेयसक्तानां मश्नूषा टिप्पणीधृवम् तत्पञ्चलक्षणीग्रन्थे व्याप्तितत्वं प्रपंचितम् सदाशिवः तवा दष्ष्टो साक्षादेव गदाधरः स चतुर्दशलक्षण्यां चातुर्यं चाप लक्षणे सिद्धान्तलक्षण प्रोक्त व्याजिसिद्धान्तमद्‌भुतं पक्षता शिक्षिता तेन क्षत पण्डित घीमता शतकोटिमुखानेक कोटिक्रमसमन्वितम् गुप्तेः सत्प्रतिप-क्षाख्यं ग्रन्थे जग्राह सूक्ष्मघीः यत्सामान्यनिरूक्तेः सा वच्छाङ्नोक्ता परिष्क्रिया व्युत्पत्तिवादे शास्त्रीयव्युत्पत्तिं प्राप्तवानसौ शक्तिवादे शब्दशक्तेः स्वरूपं महदभुतम्॥[1]

Then Sadasiva mastered the various texts in Grammar like सिद्धान्तकौमुदी, मंजूषा, मंजरी, शब्देन्दुशेखर, महाभाष्य and others;

ञवं सिद्धान्तकौमुध्यां वैशारध्यमवाप सः
वैयाकरणमंजूषा मांजस्येनावबुद्धवान्।
शब्देन्दुशेखरे चासौ चन्द्रशेखरजोयिसा
महाभाष्यस्य सौरभ्यं स्वारस्यं सरहस्यकं॥[2]

Under Sankhya he mastered सांख्यकारिका, तंत्रवार्तिक सांख्यतत्वकौमुदी In Mimamsa he was an adept in अर्थसंग्रह, मीमांसान्यायप्रकाश, आपोदेवी, शबरभाष्य, जैमिनीयन्यायमाला and in Vedanta he acquired proficiency in the Bhasyas of Sankara, Ramanuja and Madhwa.

चतुर्थस्तरङ्ग

In this Taranga, Sadasiva's visit to Kashmir, Hampi, Richness of Vijayanagar, Description of Hubli, the Sage Siddharudha, involvement in intellectual debates have been portrayed;

---

1. *Ibid.* p. 64-65
2. *Ibid.* p. 65=66

KASHMIR

Sadasiva went to Kashmir which produced intellectuals of the caliber of Abhinava Gupta, Mammata, Kalhana, Kshemendra and others;

ततः अभिनवगुप्त, मम्मट, कल्हण, क्षेमेन्द्रादि कवितल्लज कुलभवनायमानं निसर्ग सौन्दर्य समाकृष्ट सहस्राधिक वैदेशिक यात्रिक सन्दोहं काश्मीरदेशमुपजगाम।[1]

There is a graphic description of the nature of Kashmir in the following stanzas :—

कस्तूरिकांकुंकुंम केसरादि सद्वस्तु विस्तारित कीर्तिपूर्तिम्।
काश्मीरदेशस्य निसर्गशोभां स विस्मितोऽभूत् निपुणं निरीथय।
यः श्रीखण्ड शिखण्डाद्यः शशिखण्डाकपण्डितः।
स काश्मीराख्य भूखण्डः च्चुतः स्व खण्डवद् बभौ॥
उल्लोलसरितां वीची कल्लोलेस्वल्लसंत्यहो।
लसत्पुराणि काश्मीरे दृष्ट्वासौ विस्मितोऽभवत्॥[2]

HAMPI

Sadasiva also visited Hampi wherein flows the river Tunga and the great saint Vidyaranya who inhabited it;

यत्रास्ति तुङ्गा विलसत्तरङ्गा पापौदभङ्गा महिमातितुङ्गा विध्यारण्य महारण्याद् जातः शौर्य दवानलः। निर्दग्धानकरोत्सर्वान् यवनाख्यविषद्रुमान्। पम्पेत्येतत स्वनाम्नो या विपरीतं न मर्षिति पापं तस्मात्क्षणोल्लोपं पम्पा प्रापयति ध्रुवम्॥[3]

The richness of Vijayangar is graphically portrayed here;

सर्व ऽाव विजयनगरप्रदेशः तदानीं हेमकूट इव रत्नसानुरिव,

1. *Ibid.* p. 72-73
2. *Ibid.* p. 75

मणिमन्दिरमिव मौक्तिकमेरूरिव, प्रत्यभात् विजयनगरगतानि सर्वाण्यपि आयतनानि नारायणशरीराणि इव लक्ष्मी निकेतनानि आसन्। प्रतिगृहं माणिक्यकुट्टिमाः सुवर्णस्तंभाः, वैडूर्यवेदिकाः, चन्द्रकान्तचर्चितः चन्द्रशालाः, गोमेधिकालंकृता गवाक्षाः, मरकत घटितानि सोपानानि, मुक्ताजाल युवतानि मणिमण्टपानि, सूर्यकान्तसुसंपन्नाः पाठशालाः रत्नसाराणि अन्तः पुराणि संदृश्यते स्म।[१]

The entire region of Vijayanagar appeared like Hemakuta or the Mount Meru. All the houses appeared as though they are the bodies of Narayana where in Lakshmi dwells. In every house there were innumerable gems,the golden pillars and other valuables.

The poet also beautifully contrasts the past glory of Vijayanagar with the present debacle;

पूर्वं यत्र गजाः तत्र अध्य अजाः, तदा यत्र अश्वाः अध्य श्वानः, पुरा यत्र राजमहिष्यः तत्र महिष महिष्यः, पुरा यत्र गन्धर्वाः तत्र अध्य गोमायवः, पुरा यत्र सङ्गीतं तत्र अध्य गार्दभगीतम्, यत्र दम्पतीनां मधुरालापः पाक्, तत्र शिवानां घोरालापः, यत्र वेदमंत्राणां मश्रुघोषः तत्राध्य मिथः कलहायमानानां शुनां भूषण ध्वनिः शोश्रूयते, हन्त कुटिलता कालस्य, वक्रता च विधेः॥[२]

Where there was elephants now there are lambs, where horses were inhabiting now dogs lie, where the royal queens were living now the she buffalos inhabit, where the music was heard now it is the breying of the donkeys, where the pleasant vedic chanting was heard there we have the noise of the quarelling of dogs, How the times have changed and how devious the thoughts of the fate?

---

1. *Ibid.* p. 77
2. *Ibid.* p. 79

HUBLI

Sadasiva also visited Hubli which was known for its prosperity and splendor;

भूर्म्यायोज्वल नव्य निर्मित लसद्हर्म्यालि रम्यां पुरीं
चंचचंपकचूत चन्दनलता चूड़ाल लीलावनीम
पुण्यागण्यसुवर्ण नाण्य मणि मुक्ताली विपण्यान्वितां
कर्णाटि क्षिति कर्णविभ्रम मणिं हुब्बल्लिमभ्यागमत्॥[1]

DESCRIPTION OF SIDDHARUDHA

In the Siddha Ashrama an advaitic discussion was held which was presided over by Siddharudha Swamy whom Sadashiva perceived as follows;

तदा तत्र सिद्धाश्रमे आस्थानमण्डपे श्रीश्रीसिद्धारूढ़स्वामि नामाध्यक्षे प्रावर्तत अद्वैतवेदान्तगोष्ठी। तत्र समागत्य शम्भुलिङ्गेश्वरः शरीरबद्दमिव वैराग्ये, अन्तरङ्गप्रविष्टमिव अध्यात्मरहस्यां प्रदर्शनशालामिव दैवीसम्पदः, नूतन परिष्कारमिव शान्तितत्वस्य, सौभाग्यविष्कारमिव ब्रह्मतेजसः, हिमगिरि प्रदेशमिव परमेश्वरपाद पांसुपूतशिरस्कं, गङ्गाप्रवाहमिव सर्वज्ञमौलिलालितं, नारायणमिव दूरीकृत नरकभयं, अश्वत्थाममिवसर्वदा कृपानुगतं, भवानीशरीरमिव सदाक्षमनोहरं, प्रातः कालमिव उदयर-विकान्तकमनीयं, गगन मण्डलमिव आश्रितसर्वनाटकं प्रकाशपुंजमिव सकलपदार्थप्रकाशकं, शारदोत्सवमिव व्यतीतबहुवर्षं, शान्तनुराजमिव आदृतसत्यव्रतं, सिद्धिं तपसः, समृद्धिं वैराग्यस्य, महापूर दयास्रोतसः, प्रासादं प्रासादस्य, स्थानं मानस्य, तीर्थं तथ्यस्य, स्वार्थं सत्यस्य, परमार्थमध्यात्मविध्यायाः, क्षेत्रं क्षमायाः, पात्रं पावित्र्यस्य, खनित्रं आशांकुरस्य, अविषयीकृतं विषयैः, अनालोकितं कामेन, अपरिस्पृष्टं क्रोधेन, अनाघ्रतं लोभेन, उत्साहितं मात्सर्येण, दूरीकृतं दोषदानवैः, अरीकृतं आर्षगुणैः, अहंकारमोंकारस्य, भाग्यनिधिं भक्तिसीमन्तिन्याः, आहोपरुषिकां आत्मानुभवस्य, सीमारेखमिव शान्तिसाम्राज्यस्य,

1. *Ibid.* p. 79
2. *Ibid.* p. 87

विजयवैजयन्तीमिव ब्रद्धज्ञानस्य, वंध्यत्वस्यापि वन्दनीयं, पूज्यत्वस्यापि पूजनीयं, धर्मस्यापि आराधनीयं, धाम धाम्नां, मन्दिरं महिम्ना, क्षत्रं शुतितायाः, निकेतनं कौतुकस्य, सौम्यमूर्तिं भगवन्तं श्रीसिद्धारूढ़ योगीश्वरम्।[१]

There in that Siddhasrama an intellectual debate on Advaita commenced in the august presence of Siddharudha Swamy who like an embodiment of penance, the Vairagya embodied form of a person, the illustration for Daivisampath, a new form of Shanthi, an embodiment of Brahma Tejas, like Ganga to Siva, like a Narayana who has dispelled the fear of Hell, like Asvathama showing compassion to others, radiant like the rising moon, the stars to the sky, who was an embodiment of penance, a man taking form of Truth, a storehouse for tolerance, one who had never witnessed Karma, one who was never touched by anger, one who never smelt the greed, one who had vanquished the envy, one who was respectworthy even by those who are respected, one who bore always calm and serene look.

INVOLVEMENT IN INTELLECTUAL DEBATES

Shambhuinga took part in two intellectual debates of highest qualities. The first debate was with Kabirdas regarding the topic of Maya Mithyatva in Sankara Vedanta;

कबीरदासनामा विपश्चिचदपश्चिमः सुनिश्चयेन ध्वनिना वेदान्तप्रवचनं कलयन् शांकरभाष्यं विवरीषुः माया मिथ्या इति प्रत्यपादीत्। तत्क्षण ऽाव शास्त्रार्थकृतक्षणः सर्वागमविलक्षणः मेधाविलक्षणः महामनीषिलक्षण : शम्भुलिङ्गयोगीश्वरः तदसहमानः

---

1. *Ibid.* p. 89

निरभिमानः समुत्थितश्रावणाम्बर जृम्भमाणाम्योभर संभृत नवाम्बोध मदम्बरवविडंबना गम्भीरेण ध्वनिना तमाक्षिपन्नाचचक्षे धीरधीः॥[1]

The second intellectual debate was against Gurumurthy Sastri regarding चरपादप्रक्षालन पायसा पशुपतिशिरो भिषेकस्य कर्तव्यत्वविषये प्रमाणवचनम्।[2]

पञ्चमतरङ्ग

This is one of the shortest chapters where in the parents persuading Shambhulinga to take to Grihasthasrama and he refusing to accept it have been portrayed with प्रमाणवाक्य. Before this, there is a physical description of Shambhulinga also;

Physically Shambhulinga was in his Youth when he appeared as though to outbeat the charm of Manmatha. People used to think whether it is Mannatha or Sanatkumara or Skanda. He was radiant with his intellect he was like a flag of Dharma and each good quality in him appeared as though rivaling with other qualities;

तारुण्यलावण्य विलासलक्ष्मी केलीवनं यौवनमवाप शम्भुः। कन्दर्प दर्पावह रूपकान्तिं भेजे विरेजे सुहृदां समाने। अयं कुमारो ननु किं स मारः सनत्कुमारोऽत्वतवैष तस्मिन्कैश्चित् कुमारोऽसुरसंधमार इत्याशशंके सति यौवनांके।

भास्वान्स्वतेजसा दिव्ययशसा च कलाधरः धिया मन्दो गुरुर्वाचा कविगोष्ठयां सदो बुधः सकलाऽविकला ह्यस्मिन्कला ईर्ष्याकुला इव। तस्मात्कलाधरोऽयं नु नकलङ्कङ्कपङ्किलः॥[3]

Parents thought that he had attained the age of

---

1. *Ibid.* p. 90
2. *Ibid.* p. 93
3. *Ibid.* p. 100-101

marriage and the father Siddeswara told his son to marry;

तनयो विनयोपेत रसतामनुनये रतः पटुः सर्वानियेष्वध्य नूनं परिणयोचितः इति विचिंत्य ऽकान्त ऽकान्तमनोहरं तं सुकुमारं स्वकुमारमाहूय वात्सल्यास्स परिपूरितया सदिच्छाप्रेरितया तदुत्कर्ष-भावनाकारितया मोचा मधु माधुरीमुचा वाचा प्रावीवचत् सिद्धेश्वरः। तस्मादिह तवद्द्वाहं कर्तुं लघु समुत्सहे समीहे च महाकुलजकन्यया।[१]

Sadasiva replied to his parents that according to the advice of the Vedas and the Upaishads the world is transitory and hence he wants to lead the life of a Brahmacharin and he also said that it is his firm conviction not to marry;

तेषां महापुरुषाणां निगमागमौपनिषदां च निदेशानुसारेण असारमेतत्संसारं दारागारादिकं च दूरत ऽव परिहृत्य आजन्मबद्ध चर्यव्रतं आरिराधयिष्यामि तमेव द्धटरूपं परंब्रह्म। अचलोऽयं मम निर्णयः नात्र अगृण्हन्तु मां भवन्तः। परमनुगृण्हन्तु॥[२]

The mother tried to influence Shambhulinga with some of the remarks like the man without a wife is converting a house into a forest and the forest which is inhabited by a woman is the best house in all the three worlds, She further pestered him not to destroy the tower of her desires, not to destroy about her sweet dream, to fulfill her desire and her husband's desire and to think properly to give up fear and to make his pitrs to come out of a hell named puth to expand the family to lift the weight of her heart and so on;

---

1. *Ibid.* p. 101-102
2. *Ibid.* p. 105

कान्ताविरहितं पुंसां कान्तारं सदनं भवेत्। वनं च वनितायुक्तं भुवने भुवनोत्तमम्। मा चूर्णय मदीयं मनोरथमहासौधम्। मावस्कन्द सुन्दरं मम स्वप्नमन्दिरम्। पूरय मातुः चिरकांक्षितम्। निवारय पितृश्चिन्ताम्। विचारय सारासारम्। उत्सारय अनावश्यकभीतिम्। उत्तारय पितृक पुन्नाम्नो नरकात्। विस्तारय वंशम्। प्रेरय पित्राज्ञा परिपालने तव मनः। अवतारय मम हृदयभारम्।[1]

Sadasiva firm like a rock of gibṛalter replied to his mother as follows;

अम्ब, जानामि तव मनोरथम्। सहजः स्वाभाविकश्च सीमन्तिनीनां स्नुषानप्तृमुख प्रेमपुत्रलिका मुखावलोकन अकुण्ठोकण्ठभारः। स च तव मनोरथः सेस्यत्येव मदितर पुत्र परिणयेन। अहं तु स्वार्थापेक्षया परमपुरूषार्थं भीगापेक्षया योगं भाग्यापेक्षया वैराग्ये मुक्त्यपेक्षया भक्तिं, अनुरक्त्यपेक्षया मुक्तिमेव सिषाधयिषामि यावज्जन्म॥[2]

Oh mother, I know your desire. It is but natural for you to have the desire of seeing the face of a daughter in law and grand children. Your desire will be fulfilled by your other sons. But I desire to attain salvation instead of selfish ends, yoga instead of enjoyment, renunciation instead of desire, devotion instead of desires and mukti instead of love

षष्ठस्तरङ्ग

Narration of Goddess Banashankari, city Bijapur, people welcoming Swami ji have been nicely portrayed here and in these descriptions our thought naturally goes to Bana's Kadambari and Boja's Champu Ramayana;

GODDESS BANASHANKARI

तत्र देवस्थानस्य परिस्थितायाा तट स्फुरन्नवनलिन पुरनिष्छयूत

1. *Ibid.* p. 106-107
2. *Ibid.* p. 108

मधुपान लम्पट षट्पद परली पापठ्यमानोंकार शंकावहझंकार मनोहारिण्यां शैवालबाहुल्यतया हरिद्वु र्णपयोधारिण्यां पुष्करिण्यां प्रक्षाल्य पाणिपादं गर्भागारं प्रविश्य ददर्श भगवतीं नग राजतनया जगदण्डमण्डल-निर्माण शौण्डीर खण्डपरशु नयनपुण्डरीक भमद् भ्रमरायमाणचेतस्कां वनस्थलीमिव सिंहाधिष्ठितां, काव्यपद्धतिमिव सर्गोपसर्ग निर्माणचतुरां, असुरसाम्राज्यश्रियमिव कविप्रवराभिनन्दितां, कमलिनीमिव वनान्तरोप-शोभिनां, महानसस्थलीमिव भक्तसंकुलां रविप्रभामिव साधितोदयां हरिननावतीमिव कृपानुगृहीत धृतराष्ट्रां, यागिचित्त कृपानुगृहीत धृतराष्ट्रां, योगचित्त प्रवृत्तिमिव गृहीत विषमाक्षां, कादम्बिनीमिव नील-कण्ठहृदयाह्लादिनी, प्रभातसंध्यामिव कुंकुमकान्तिकमनीयां, वन-स्थलीमिव द्विजश्रुतिघोष मुखरितोपान्ता जीवप्रवृत्तिमिव भवानुरागबद्धाम्, भागवतकथामिव स्कन्दानन्दसन्दायिनीं, सुरासर मुकुटीतटिघत्ति हारिहीर-ज्योतिर्नीराजित पादपल्लवां, जगज्जन्मस्थेम प्रत्यवहार कारपीभूतां, सर्वोद्धारिणीं, जगदनिष्टा पापकदृष्टा भ्रष्ठ पापिष्ठ दनुजकुल संहारिणीं संसार सागर समुत्तारिणीं, खड्गत्रिशूलादि धोटायुधधारिणीं, समस्त क्षमाक्षेमकरीं रिपुकुलभयंकरीं शिवकिंकरीं बनशंकरीं ददर्श॥[१]

In that beautiful land of abounding nature where bees were humming, he saw the goddess Banashankari whose eyes were like that of a lotus, who was seated on a lion, who was like a lotus enriching the beauty of the forest, radiant like the rays of sun, whose mind was like that of the yogins, who was like parvati to siva, who was wearing a Kumkum on her forehead which resembled the morning sun, who is the creator, sustainer and destroyer of the world, who is the dispeller of darkness and the evil demons, who makes people to cross over this ocean in the form of bondage, who is the wielder of the fierce weapons like a sword, trident and others, who does good to the entire humanity, who is fierce to the enemies.

1. *Ibid.* p. 114-115

CITY OF BIJAPUR

Shambulinga entered Bijapur which was as follows;

ततस्तथैव सर्वकर्तुः शर्वस्व सर्वकारणेन प्रेरणेन प्रचोदितः बिल्ववनं परित्यज्य श्रीशिवाचार्य हुणशीकट्टिमागतिः मुण्डगन्नासमीपे नदीमुत्तीर्य बदरीग्रामेत्वेकदिनमुषित्वा कर्णाटिकेऽतिप्रसिद्धं चिरकालं पुरा यवनभूपाल अल्लेआदिलशाहादि शासनं गोलगुम्मटादि विश्वविस्मापक वास्तुशिल्प वैभव ध्योतक मन्दिर समाधि मसीदादि शोभते विजयपुरं नाम नगरम् समुपासदत॥[1]

Then according to the inspiration having left Bilavana, Sri Shambhulinga by way of hunasikatti crossing the river near Mandagam and stayed for a day in Bidar village came to Bijapur which is very well known in Karnataka where in for a long time the muslim ruler Ali Adil Shahi ruled and where in we have the architectural splendour like Gol Gumbaz;

PEOPLE'S REACTION TO THE ARRIVAL OF THE SWAMIJI

The happy reaction of the people on seeing Swamiji here has a parallel to Dasaratha's announcement in Champu Ramayana that he is going to coronate Rama as his successor;

विजयन्तां पंचाचार्याः विजयन्तां श्रीशम्भुलिङ्ग शिवाचार्याः, वर्धतां वीरशैवमतं, समुध्यतां बृहन्मठः, जेगीयतां शिवयोगीश्वरः, इत्यादि सुरभाषामयैश्च जयघोषैः सामाड़ैः सोत्साद महापूरैः स्वोल्लस्वमुच्चरितैः। जयशब्दकलकल कोलाहलैश्च मुखरीकुर्वन्ति दिङ्मुखानि। बधिरीकुर्वन्तो दम्भोलिपाणि कुम्भीन्द्रस्याणि कर्णकुम्भाम्बरविवरं। भाविस्व मठाधिपतीन् श्रीशिवाचार्यान् आन्दोलिक्यामुपवेश्य अहमहमिकया पर्यायेण

1. *Ibid.* p. 125

सोत्साहं वहन्तः विजयपुरस्य प्रमुखवीथिषु घण्ठापथं च संचारयन्तः बीजापुरस्य जोशपूर विभागस्थित बृहन्मठं समुपाजग्मुः सादरप्रमोदभर भेदरितमानसाः।[१]

Let victory come to Panchacharyas, let Shambhulinga Sivacharya be victorious, let the Veerasaiva faith spread such were the loud enthusiastic sounds which had filled the air and that sound was deafening the ears and they took the future swamiji of the Mutt in the palanquin turns with all eagerness in the main roads of Bijapur and finally entered the Brihanmatha with their mind full of devotion and respect towards the Swamiji.

सप्तमस्तरङ्ग

देशाटन, शोभायात्र and back to bijapur are the subjects dealt with here;

ऽवं गच्छंत्यां कियत्यामपि कलकलायां शिष्यजन प्रार्थनानुसारेण सञ्चरन्तः। तत्र तत्र परिहरन्तः भक्तचिन्ताम्, उद्धरन्तः दीनदलितान्, वितरन्तः प्रसादं, विकिरन्त दयामतशीकरान्। विहरन्तः शिवमत्तिरसोदधौ। स्फुरन्त इव बालसूर्याः, चरन्त इव गुरूकरूणाः, तटन्त इव भवसिन्धुं, सरन्त इव शिवमूर्तयः श्री शम्भूलिङ्गशिवाचार्याः कर्णाटक सीमा प्रान्त सप्रल्लससि, समुत्सप्रल्लससि नैकशिवभक्ततल्लज परिकुल्लं, सोल्लापुरं नाम नगरं समुपाजग्मुः।[२]

Shambhulinga entered Sholapur and that is portrayed here; Traveling from place to place according to the desire of the disciples Sri Shambhulinga by dispelling the misery of the devotees, by doing good to the poor and the needy, shining like an infant Sun, as though a bridge to cross the miseries crossed the border of Karnataka and reached Sholapur.

1. *Ibid.* p. 131
2. *Ibid.* p. 142

शोभायात्रा

This shows the respect which Swamiji commanded;

राजधान्याः प्रमुखवीथीषु प्रावर्तत शोभायात्रा श्रीशिवाचार्याणाम्। अग्रे कादली, ढक्का, भेरी, आनक, गोमुखादयः। ततो मुश्चल तूर्यस्वन। वेणु, सारङ्गी, मुख मङ्गलवाध्यवृन्दः, तदनु समवस्त्रधारिणाः, तालबद्धपद्धतौ त्वरितक्रमेण सरभस पदतल प्रत्क्षेपोक्षेप पुरस्सरं चलन्तः, रक्षापुरुषाः, तत्पश्चात् चंचल्लचलाचामीकर चारूचन्द्रहासान् हस्तेषु उध्यम्य चंचलासंचयमिव संचालयन्तः, सैनिकपुरुषाः, तदनु शुभ्रस्वच्छ-तरोचैश्राव सन्दोह सन्देह सन्दायक सिन्धुरवृन्द समारूढ़ सादिश्रेरणी, तत्पश्चात् गायकाः, नर्तकाः, पूर्णकुंम्भ धारिणः, मंत्रघोषं कुर्वाणः पुरोहिताः, मङ्गलकलश कुंकमक्कण्डकदर्पण लाजाक्षतहस्ताः, सुवा-सिन्यः, संस्थानगजराजौ, ततो नादिदूरे ठव पुष्पमालालंकृते मुक्तादाम स्तोमाभिरामे राजद्वल्ललरारिज विराजि ज्योतिः पुत्र्य नीराजिते सूर्यरथनन्दने मन्दमन्द स्पन्दने चन्दनमये शङ्गारिते राजष्यन्दने समुपविष्टाः वैराग्यमूर्तयः श्री शम्भुलिङ्गशिवाचार्याः तत्पश्चात् परः सहस्राः जयघोषं कुवणिाः नागरिकाः नराः नार्यश्च शनैः शनैः प्रचलतिस्म शोभायात्रायाम्॥[1]

People had gathered on the main streets to greet Sri Sivacharya. In the front there was the sound of Drum, Conch, Lute, Sarangi and other instruments, then and there were people in uniform who were marching majestically, then the military, then singers, dancers and priests chanting Vedas with poorna Kumba in their hands to welcome him, then the chaste women with the Kumkum in their hands then the elephants and finally Sri Sivacharya being followed by thousands of devotees.

BACK TO BIJAPUR

Then Sri Sivacharya came back to Bijapur and a royal welcome awaited him there also;

1. *Ibid.* p. 144

सर्वत्र विजयन शैववैजयन्तीं समुद्रधवन्
विजयाख्यापुरं प्रायात शम्भुलिङ्गशिवः सुधीः।
विजापुरप्रजाः सर्वाः प्रजापतिमिवामराः
संसभ्रमसमारम्भं नेमुः शम्भुगुरोत्तमम्।
मुहुर्दर्शं दर्शं यतिततिपते भास्वखपुः।
अहो श्रावं श्रावं सरसमुपदेशं प्रतिदिनम्।
सदा पायं पायं तदमलवचः स्वादिमसुधां
विजापुराभिख्या समधिकमदापुरि च पुरी॥[१]

All the people of Bijapur bowed down to revered Swamiji with great respect and enthusiasm. Having seen the sacred form of Swamiji and having listened to his discourses daily and having drank his sweet words the people of Bijapur were immensely happy.

अष्टमस्तरङ्ग

The glory of river Krishna, the description of the nature are the prominent topics in this chapter. The glory of Krishna river is described in sixty stanzas out of which some may be mentioned here from the point of view of the style of the poet and the felicity of expression.

GLORY OF RIVER KRISHNA

विधात्री क्षेमाणां सकलजनधात्री सकरूणा प्रदात्री कामानां सलिलमयगात्री शुचिकरी नियंत्री चोरानां जगति विनिहंत्री च विपदाम् इयं कृष्णांगात्था विमलयतु कृष्णा सपदिमाम्। सकृत्कृष्णास्नानं जनिमरणहानं प्रकुरूते सकृत्कृष्णापानं परिहरति दैनन्दिन शुचः सकृत्कृष्णाहानं क्षपयति यमाह्वानजभयम् मनः कृष्णालंकादयति खलु

1. *Ibid.* p. 158

कृष्णांघ्रिकमलम्। काशीं नाहमयासिषं न च मयायोध्या गयाध्यासिषि कांचीं किंचन गन्तुमिच्छति मनो द्वारावतीं नाक्षति नान्यत्पुष्करमुख्य पुष्कल महाक्षेत्राग्रय तीर्थाव्यगांर्था कृष्णे त्वत्करूणाकणैक शरणस्तीरोऽस्मि मां तारय[1]।

The bestower of contentment, the fulfiller of the desires, the one with pure water, the dispeller of the obstacles let that Krishna purify me.

If we take bath in Krishna once, all our births and deaths will be dispelled, if we sip a drop of water from the river krishna, we will be clean and pure in our approach.

I did not visit Kashi, Ayodhya, Kanchi, Dwaravathi, Pushkar and other holy centres, but, Oh krishna, I am totally surrendering myself before you, please protect me.

Ramalingappa a devotee asked the people where he could build a hermitage for the Swamiji and here we find beautiful description of nature;

जम्बूखण्ड़ीतिनेदिष्ठ भूखण्डाग्नेयादिकूटे काननान्तः प्रदेशान्त वेशिन्तोऽस्ति प्रशान्तिभूः। तत्तीरे विलसन्नीरे लोलहानीरलालिते शिवालयोपि बाभाति शोभालाभोन्नती भुवि। श्रीगन्ध बन्दु माकन्द पिचुमन्द है वृन्दतः निष्यन्दमकरन्दार्द्र सौगन्धामन्द नन्दनम्। जम्बू जम्बीर निम्बोच्चै रम्भादि द्रुक्दम्बितं कदम्बादि कदम्बाति सम्बाध शिशिरान्तरम् स्वच्छोदं नामनोच्छोदं किं जलाजीर्णतः सरः।[2]

There is a calm place in the forest near Jambukandi where there is a beautiful Siva temple which is surrounded by trees like Sandal, Bandhu, Makanda, Pichumanda, Nisyanda, Makaranda, Jambu Jambira,

1. *Ibid.* p. 226-228
2. *Ibid.* p. 241

Nimba, Rambha, Kadamba and others and there is also a lake named Acchoda. This brings us to our memory the description of Acchoda lake in Bana's Kadambari.

नवमस्तरङ्ग

Here the style of Shambhulinga's discourses is nicely narrated;

श्री श्री शम्भुलिङ्गशिवाचार्य महास्वामिनां सरस सुन्दरं, भावबन्धुरं, वैरस्यविधुरं, शास्त्रसर्वकंषं, निगमागम कुलंकषं, सुश्राव्यं पण्डितानां, मनोरंजकं पामराणां, मार्गदर्शकं महिलामणीनां, बोधप्रदं ब्राह्मणानां, स्फूर्तिपादकं वीरशैवानां, दुगुन्मीलकं विध्यार्थिनां, श्रद्धेयं विध्योपजीविनां, तृप्तिदायकं तत्वबुभुत्सूनां, परनिवृतिप्रापकं रसिकानां, समाधायकं वैज्ञानिक यक्षप्रश्नानां, उद्धारकं ज्ञानभण्डारस्य, पारदर्शकं सारस्वत महोदधेः, गोष्यस्फोटकं अध्यात्मरहस्याणां, अनावरणमहोत्सवं वैदिक-वाङ्मयगकड़ार्यानां, मर्मोद्घाटकं वचनशास्त्रप्रमेयाणां, प्रत्यादेशं नास्तिक-विचाराणां, समुचितोत्तरं पाखण्डिपूर्वपक्षाणां, समन्वय मार्गदर्शकं सर्वधर्माणाम्, दिक्सूचकं वर्णसमासस्य, पथप्रदर्शकं जातिबान्धवस्य, निवारणकारणं मिथोमतवैषम्यस्य, परिहारसूत्रं पारस्परिकमतिवैमनस्यस्य, सुवर्णसेतुभूतं सर्वजातीय स्नेहसागरस्य, अमन्दानन्द सन्दायकं अध्याप-कानां, बह्मानन्ददं तत्वजिज्ञासूनां, आह्लादकं श्रोत्रुसामान्यस्य आत्या-यकमतजनानां, अत्यादराकर्ण्यं प्राज्ञ पुङ्गवानां, विषयविषयोपधापकं विमर्शकानां, संशयच्छेदकं विचिकित्सूनां, सध्योविभेदकं हृदयग्रन्थीनां, मोदकं अविपालगोपाल स्त्रीशूद्रप्रद्विज बन्धूनां, विविधविषय प्रतिपादकं, विश्वजनबोधकं, दिव्यतत्व साधकं, परमेश्वर पारम्य निवेदकं, वीरशैवमत विशिष्टोपपादकं च प्रवचनं सर्वजनाकर्षकं प्राचलत।[१]

Sri Shambhulinga Swamiji's discourses were filled with emotion, bereft of quarrels, the essence of all the Sastras, the purport of Veda, melodious to the scholars,

---

1. *Ibid.* p. 210

entertainment for the layman, torch bearers for ladies, Kindling interest in the brahmins, encouraging to the Veerasaivas, and eye- opener for the students, contentment for the philosophers, salvation for the connoisseurs, an answer to all the scientific question, an opener to the key of knowledge, an imagination to the hidden meanings of Vedic words, and answer to the heterodox people, an answer to all the wicked people, a harmony for all the religions, a trend setter for the equanimity of castes, for the harmony of religions a golden bridge, causing immense delight to the teachers, a Brahmananda to the philosophers, respectworthy for the scholars, a new thought for the critics, dispeller of all doubts to students, depicting different themes, revealing the nature of God, and depicting the basic tenets of Veerasaivism.

दशमस्तरङ्ग

Teaching the basic Sanskrit texts to Chidananda and curing the deadly diseases are nicely portrayed here;

काव्योपनिषदं प्रौढ़ं नैषधं विद्वदौषधम् शिशुपालवधं काव्यमशिक्षिष्ट निरूपयत कुमारसंभवं यत्र शाम्भवे मारमाराणम मेघदूतरसमेघ निः सरद कादम्बरीगद्यप्रबन्धं काव्यादर्शं कुमाराणां, उत्तरं रामचरितं भवभूत्युत्तमां कृतिम्, गीतगोविन्द सौन्दर्यलहरीमुख्याः क्षीरब्ध्यूर्मिर्विजित्वरीः सानन्दं कुवलयानन्दं ध्वन्यालोकमध्यापयन रसगङ्गाधरादर्थशगा शूभुं भगीरथः काव्यप्रकाशसद्ग्रन्थ मुदग्रन्थग्रन्थिरूपिणम्॥[1]

Shambhlinga Swamy taught Naishada, Sisupalavadha, Kumarasambhava, Meghaduta, Kadambari, Kavyadarsha, Uttara Rama charita, Gita Govinda, Soun-

1. *Ibid.* p. 226-228

darya lahari, Kuvalayananda, Dhvanyaloka, Rasagangadhara, Kavyaprakasha, and other basic Sanskrit texts to Chidananda.

Shambhulinga Swamiji cured a child who was suffering from deadly diseases;

तां च तथाविधं रूग्णशिशुं गृहीत्वा गच्छन्तीं स्थविरामाकार्य स्वसमीपमानय्य श्रीशम्भुलिङ्ग शिवाचार्यवर्यः तस्य शिशोर्व्याधिवर्धितं शरीरं सकरूणं सानुग्रहं च वरदहस्तेनाममर्श।[1]

Having invited an old lady who was carrying a child ridden with a disease Shambhulinga Swamy touched the body of the child with his hand and the child became normal.

एकादशस्तरङ्ग

This is also one of the short chapters wherein Swamiji making a poorman rich and granting an issue out of his power is nicely portrayed;

यदा लक्ष्मीकटाक्षालक्षितात्वं भविष्यसि लक्षाधीशः तदा त्वत्तः स्वीकरिष्यामि दक्षिणाम्। तेषां वाणी मधुद्रोणी सुधा वीच्यनहारिणी कथंकारं नु मिथ्यात्वं गाहतां व्याहतार्थताम्॥[2]

When a devotee Lingaraj tried to offer some money to Swamiji, Swamiji said I will take it when You become a millionaire and how can the words of Swamiji become false and he did become a millionaire.

And when Lingaraj prayed for a child in front of Swamiji, he got a child also with the grace of Swamiji;

एवमनेकविधा सेवाशुश्रूषा विधाविधानैः सुप्रसन्नेषु श्रीचरणेषु लिङ्गराजमहोदयः स्वस्य सुतानामाकांक्षां प्रकटीचकार। ततः कतिपयैरेवा-होभिरहो फलग्राहि समभूदस्य मनोरथः। कन्दर्पसुन्दरः नन्दनः सञ्जातः।[3]

1. *Ibid.* p. 241
2. *Ibid.* p. 252
3. *Ibid.* p. 253

Thus even in this chapter like the previous chapter some of the humanitarian benevolent acts of Shambhulinga Swamy have been narrated.

द्वादशस्तरङ्ग

Trying to attack Swamiji as a consequence succumbing to a disease, the works of Swamiji,and the praise of Swamiji have been narrated in this concluding chapter;

When a fool to kill Swamiji approached him, on account of the divine power of Swamiji that person succumbed to दुमरिण.

THE WORKS OF SWAMIJI

श्री गुरुत्तमैः विरचिताः वीरशैवसिद्धान्तप्रवेशः, अष्टावरणविवेकः, महिम्नस्तवटीका, आगम परिज्ञानम्, वेदपरिचयः, वैदिकवाङ्मय रहस्यम्, शिवशक्तिविलासः, शिवशक्ति- विलासः, तत्वज्ञानं, गोरक्षणं निजमुक्तित्रिपदी, बोधारत्नाकरः, शिवपूजाविधिः, निरंजनशतक व्याख्यानप्रभृतयः।[१]

Revered Swamiji wrote number of works like Veerasaiva siddhanta pravesha, Astavarana Viveka, Mahimnastavatika, Agama pari jnanam, Veda parichayah, Vaidika Vangmaya Rahasyam, Sivashakti Vilasa, Tattvajnanam, Gorakshanam, Nijamukti Tripadi, Bodharatnakara, Sivapuja Vidhi Niranjana Shataka and others.

PRAISE OF SWAMIJI

पूज्यपादाः अक्षपात्रं ज्ञानान्नवितरणस्य। उत्पत्तिः निगमागमानाम्। विजयपताकां ज्ञानोपलब्ध्या धवलकीर्तिः। यज्ञेन्दुदुन्दुभिर्विद्यादिग्विजयस्य।

---

1. *Ibid.* p. 279

कल्पद्रुमो भरताभीष्टसम्पूर्तेः। रत्नाकरो माधुयस्यि। कोमलता कुसुमस्य। निर्माल्यता मन्दाकिनीशीतल सलिलशीकराणाम्। रमणीयता रजनीनाथस्य। अगधात्वं सरित्पतेः। समता वसुन्धरायाः। द्रवता जीवनस्य। सत्वं ब्रह्मचर्यस्य। शान्तिरूडुपतेः। गम्भीरता महार्णवस्य। प्रखरध्युतिः दशशतदीधितेः। पंचाननो विषयमृगाणाम्। शम्भो धार्मदूषणोन्मंत्र द्विरदगण्डभेदस्य। भूतनाथः समस्तभूतगण समुद्धरणस्य। अस्ताचलो अधर्मस्य। मार्तण्ड़ः सद्धर्मानुसरणस्य। चपलता गरुत्मतः। प्रसन्नता सुरेन्द्रापवनस्य। रमणीयता सृष्टेः। धवलता विशुद्धवृत्तेः। दीपकः सन्मार्गस्य। दिनकरो आज्ञानध्वान्तस्य। गुरुरपवर्गप्राप्तेः। परमध्युतिर्जीवलोकस्य। दिव्यौषधिः जीवनान्धमयस्य। आधारयष्टिः हिमशैलराज तनयाकान्त दिव्यदर्शनस्य। सद्गुरुरविध्याप्रभ पलनदीक्षायाः। परशुवसिनाद्रुमस्य। उगमो विश्वास सौहार्दस्य। निवासः सच्चिदानन्दपरशिवस्य।[१]

Sri Shambhulinga Swamiji was like an Akshayapatra in delivering the food in the form of knowledge. He was the abode of Vedas and Upanishads. He was like a banner for knowledge. He was like a Kalpa Vruksha to the devotees. He was as sacred as the waters of the river Ganges. He was as delightful as that of a moon. He had tolerance like mother earth. He had the power of Brahmacharya and the calmness of a moon.He was as majestic as a ocean. He was as radiant as hundred sons. He was like a lion to the armies in the form of senses, He was like a sunset to Adharma. He had the pleasantness of creation. He was a torch bearer for riteousness. He was like a Sun god dispelling ignorance. He was like a giver of salvation. He was like a divine medicine to all the human beings. He was like a path to see Siva. He was a teacher to the Knowledge. He was like an axe to the physical senses. He was the root cause for harmony and confidence and he was an abode of Siva himself.

1. *Ibid.* p. 286

CONCLUSION

Thus , apart from its historical value it is a fine poetic composition. Sri Pandarinathacharya is a gifted contemporary Sanskrit Poet. He has a fine capacity to manipulate a rhythm of sound in Sanskrit poetry and prose which captures the listeners. Following the traditional style of prose and champu in Sanskrit he has introduced many Alankaras like श्लेष, उपमा, उत्प्रेक्षा, विरोधाभास, उल्लेख etc and metres like शार्दूलविक्रीडित रथोद्धता, अनुष्टुप्, इन्द्रवज्र, वसन्ततिलका, द्रुतविलम्बिता, वियोगिनी etc in an effective way. His vast knowledge of Itihasas, Puranas and Sanskrit classics has enabled him to introduce many lierary and cultural forms which are not only delightful but give a fund of information about our culture and tradition. While describing the education of Sadasiva he almost gives a brief history of Sanskrit Liteature and mentions major writers on poetics and Sastras. He introduces a few Philosophical dialogues and discussions about Veerasaiva tenets while describing the meeting with scholars. A Short poem on river Krisna is incorporated while describing that river. Thus, this work is at once a history, a poem, a philosophical work, and a charming presentation of the spiritual life of a scholar, and a saint. A subtle humour is also introduced here and there giving a relief to the seriousness of the theme and one may mention in passing that this is also an award winning work.

6

PRAHLADA CHAMPU-KANARADI VITTALOPADHYAYA-1989.

Prahlada Champu by Kanaradi Vittalopadhyaya was published in the year 1989 by Akhila Karnataka Samskruta Parishad, Kundapura. An attempt has been made here to highlight some of the significant points presented in this Champu as a sample survey. The author commences the work on a traditional note with a मङ्गलाचरण to Lord Narasimha in keeping with the subject matter;

श्रीमन्नृकण्ठीरवकण्ठलग्ना मालामलाबालक कण्ठलग्ना।।
प्रह्लादमाह्लादयतु प्रबुद्धा प्राणान्तसूत्रेण हिरण्यजग्धेः।।[1]

This stanza composed in इन्द्रवज्रा metre has a beautiful alliteration.

We have a fine alliteration in the nineteenth stanza;

विश्वसृड़ाध्या विबुधा विष्णुपदे विष्वगमुम्।
वीक्षितुमाविश्य रणं विस्मितचित्तेद्धभवन्।।[2]

1. Prahlada Champu-Kanaradi Vittalopadhyaya-Akhila Karnataka Samskruta Parishat, Kundapur, 1989, p. I.
2. *Ibid.* p. 8

Stanza twenty seven could be taken as an illustration for युग्मक;

इति बालकरूपधरं शमने, शमनन्तशरीखतां ददतम्।
ददतं नृपबन्धुजनाः प्रमितिं प्रमितिह्यगताः प्रययुः शरणम्॥[1]

Prahlada's address to the Lord is nicely brought out by the poet with a nice balance of words;

अपि पितः पितामहस्यापि पितरं, शिवस्यापि शिवंकरं, सुरपतेरपि परं, पतिमीद्वश्वरस्यामधीश्वरं, सुरद्विषामतिशय द्विषं, वेदवेदाङ्गाध्यखिल विध्यासुवेध्यं, निखद्यं, तमादिमध्यान्त हीनमेवैनं जनार्दनं समन्ततो ममान्तर्बहिः शरीरस्य पश्यतो मे नान्यदस्ति विध्यया लभ्यम्॥[2]

What is the use of knowledge to me when I am perceiving You who are a father even to a father, an auspicious one even to Siva, greater than Indra, a substratum even to Isvara, the supreme knower of the Vedas and Vedangas, one who is bereft of the beginning and the end;

There is a fine शब्दचमत्कार in stanza ninety six;

कनककशिपुसूनुना काननाभ्यन्तरे विश्वतः
श्रुतिकठिनमहो समुत्थं च तप्वुब्दजालं श्रुतम्।
छटछटछटिलेति कमरिपूर्वप्रभूतै रवै
धुलिध्रुलर्घ्रलनिःस्वनो यां झरंऽन्यैः समं दूरतः॥[3]

Here the expression कनककशिपुसूनु for प्रह्लाद is an unusual one.

The आदिप्रास in the stanza 106 is admirably brought out by the poet;

1. *Ibid.* p. 11
2. *Ibid.* p. 22
3. *Ibid.* p. 38

राचिचर रात्रिचर रेऽत्र विपिनोऽमुं
संत्यजत संन्यजत हिंस्रमृगमध्ये।
बाघयतु भक्षयतु पञ्चनखमुख्य
दूश्चारततिकेनमिति चाह मृगवार॥[1]

Again, we have nice alliteration in the stanza 122;

अर्चामर्चितुमर्चिकोऽथं निलये काल्या परीतो भटैः
भलिनीलमणिप्रवालरचितां द्राक्षमालां गले।
घण्टाशंखकमण्डलूस्तत इतश्चास्ते प्रधानाश्चरना
सन्नद्धः सततं करालवदनः कौशेयरक्ताम्बरः॥[2]

The poet is an expert in using युग्मक not only in poetry but also in prose;

कथमिव कथयामि यामिनीचरनाथादि मेपितः स अनाथपाता पीताम्बरधरोऽन्तर्बहिश्च धरां व्यात्यान्तर्हितोप्यस्माकं हितमेव साधायन्नध स्तादुपरिष्ठान्सर्वतश्चेति दशसु काष्ठास्वप्यणुरेणु तृणाकाष्ठादिकमारभ्य जगत्स्रष्टारं स्रष्टारं जगच्चाव्याप्त विध्यमानास्वच्युत मन्यमान्ये वान्यस्मिन्कस्मिन्नुपि न विध्यत इति॥[3]

When हिरण्यकशिपु was killed by the Lord the divine trees showered flowers, the divine ladies and the divine sages came there at once to perceive the sight;

स्ररतस्सुमनोभिवर्षणं सुखनिताश्च ववर्षुस्तसुकाः।
सुरमुनिगणदेवतायुताः सुरसदृशाः सहस्राव्रजंस्तदा॥[4]

We have a reference to the name of the poet and the beauty of the work in the last stanza;

सुहृद्यैर्गध्यैः संकलितरुचिरै स्र्व्यावृतानेकवृत्तः
समेतां संख्याभिर्विठल इति कविः श्रेयासे तन्मुदन्ते।

1. *Ibid.* p. 42-43
2. *Ibid.* p. 50
3. *Ibid.* p. 58
4. *Ibid.* p. 63

यथाशक्त्यङ्गेष्वाभरणवसनै र्भूषितां चाषिचम्पूं
पितायोषां पूर्णामिव नववरे बद्धरणीमां नियुंक्ते॥[1]

The poet Vittalopadhyaya has decked this work with a beautiful prose and verses with variegated metres and has offered it at the feet of the Lord.

At this stage, it may be interesting to note the variety of metres used here. The poet in toto has made use of fifty nine metres; इन्द्रवज्रा stanzas 68, III, शार्दूलविक्रीड़ित stanzas 61, 122, उपेन्द्रवज्रा stanzas 65, 138, मालिनी Stanzas 72, 128, स्रग्धरा Stanzas 23, 115, वंशस्थ Stanzas 73, 112, अनुष्टुप् Stanzas 55, 137, स्वागता Stanzas58, 125, मेघविस्फूर्जिता Stanzas 80, 162, दोधक Stanzas 32, 105 stanzas 80, 162, stanzas 32, 105, प्रमिताक्षरा stanzas 62, 117, भुजङ्गप्रयात stanzas 77, 113, प्रमापिका stanzas 68, 254, द्रुतविलम्बिता stanzas63, 123, अतिशायिनी stanzas 101, 143, वियोगिनी stanzas 60, प्रहर्षिणी stanzas 71, 127, माणवकम् stanzas 76, पृथ्वी stanzas 98, 144, रूचिरा stanzas 66, 125, भ्रमरविलसित stanzas 84, 152, उपजाति stanzas 70, 126, मत्तमयूर stanzas 89, 152, तीटक stanzas 59, 118, प्रमुदितवदना stanzas65, 141, वैश्वदेवी stanzas 78, 114, जलोद्धतगति stanzas 87, 135, उद्गता stanzas 97, 155, स्रग्विणी stanzas 87, 135, मन्दाक्रान्ता stanzas 101, 148, प्रभा stanzas 88, 136, शालिनी stanzas, 57, 110, पञ्चकावली stanzas 86, 149, क्षमा stanzas 56, 132, हरिणी stanzas 108, 124 आर्यागीति stanzas74, 141, शिखरिणी stanzas 91, 140, महामालिनी stanzas 96, 150, रथोद्दता stanzas 91, 120, जागतमिन्द्रवंशा stanzas 79, 139, जलधारमाला stanzas 52, 121, वंशपत्रपति stanzas 64, 142, कुटजा stanzas 92, 131, पुष्पिताग्रा stanzas 60, 161, अपरवक्त्रम् stanzas 82, 153, औपच्छन्दसिकम्

1. *Ibid.* p. 67

stanzas 86, 103, प्रच्चा stanzas 85, 130, कुरटीस्चा stanzas 145, 156, ऋषभगति stanzas 104 इन्द्रवज्रा stanzas 106, 160, and वातोर्मि stanzas 107, 149

To conclude one may say that though the theme is Mythological the way the poet has dealt with the subject matter, there is novelty in it. The total command of the poet over the शब्दार्थालंकार and even some of the unusual metres is admirable. The poet seems to have a fancy for अनुप्रास and युग्मक.

7

TEERTHARAJA CHAMPU ABHIRAJA RAJENDRA MISHRA

This is a Champu which highlights the greatness of prayag (Teertharaja) written by Abhiraja Dr.Rajendra Mishra who hails from that place. This is the second Champu in his collection of five Champus entitled Abhiraja Champu. This Champu highlights an introduction to Uttar Pradesh, its serene atmosphere, the relation of the life of Kalidasa with Prayag, the holy Bharadhwaja hermitage, the commingling point or rivers Ganga and Yamuna, the association of the dynasties like Kalachuris, Guptas, Moghuls, Lodhis etc, the important personalities and our political leaders like Kumarila Bhatta, Vallabha, Chaitanya, Madan Mohan Malaviya, Motilal Nehru, Jawaharlal Nehru, Indira Gandhi, Lal Bahadur Sastri, the University of Allahabad which is termed as the Oriental Cambridge, the unique Mahakumbha Ceremony which is held once in twelve years and so on with nice appropriate alankaras like Upama, Malopama, Virodhabhasa, Anuprasa etc. Then and there one can see the influence of Bana's Kadambari in respect to the style of the poet and in this background an attempt is made in the following pages to highlight some of the significant points present in the Champu as a sample survey.

The learned poet commences his work with an introduction to Uttar Pradesh which serves as a fitting background before narrating Prayag and which is embedded with a nice Virodhabhasa Alankara;

अस्ति वृन्दारक निकुम्बसततानुगीत प्रशस्तिके हिमवर्षाजनाभवर्षापरसंज्ञे भारतवर्षे सुरसिन्धु कलिन्द नन्दिनीसरयूगोमती नारायणी चर्मण्वती वेत्रवती तमसा शोणभद्रकौशिकी सलिलाभिषेचन सस्यश्यामल, शीर्षाहित तुहिनाचल धावलकिरीटोऽपि तपोवनपर्याकुलः, प्रतिपदमेव भवभवानीसिन्धु रास्यराघव यादवांजनेय मतस्यालय प्रचुरतया देवभातृकोपयदेवमातृकः, मध्य प्रदेशथ्यन्तरानुप्रविष्ट धारित्रीलाङ्गलोऽपि वरहितलाङ्गूलः, शीर्षाधिाष्ठित बदरीकेदारो प्यबदरीकेदारः, प्रातिवेशिकीकृत विहारो प्यविहारः, परितो व्याकीर्ण कौशाम्बी काम्पिल्य हस्तिनापुर श्रावस्तीकपिलवस्तु वरणावतेष्वाह कान्यकुब्जप्रभृति भग्नावशेषोप्यभग्नावशेषः। हिमगिरि विंध्याचलाभ्यां सप्रश्रयं श्रेडीकृतोप्यक्रोड़ः। प्रागतनार्यावर्त पदवाच्चो भारतीयराज्येषु श्रेष्ठो गरिष्ठो महिष्ठोऽथ वरिष्ठो भूखण्डलरत्नभूतः उत्तर प्रदेशः।

Uttara Pradesh is endowed with many life giving rivers like Sindhu, Saraya, Gomathi, Vetravathi, Tamasa, Koushiki,and others. We can note here that some of the above mentioned rivers like Tamasa, Sarayu have found mention in the Adikavya Ramayana also. Infact Ramayana composition gets inspiration on the holy banks of Tamasa only wherein Valmiki curses the hunter when the hunter had shot one of the Krouncha birds.

मा निषाद प्रतिष्ठां त्वमगमः शाश्वतीः समाः।
यत्कौंच मिथुनादेकं अवधीः काममोहितम्॥

We have a fine poetic exaggeration in the statement शीर्षाहित तुहिनाचल धवलकिरीट wherein one can note the prowess of Rajendra Mishra over apt exaggerations.

A FINE VIRODHABHASA ALANKARA

A fine Virodhabhasa Alankara has been introduced in some of the following statements like, देवमातृकोप्यदेवमातृक:, मध्यप्रदेशाश्चन्तरानुप्राविष्ट धरित्रीलाङ्गूलोऽपि विरहितलाङ्गूल:, शीर्षाधिाष्ठित बदरीकेदारोप्यबदरीकेदार: प्रातिवेशिकीकृत विहारोप्यविहार: and so on.

Next, the learned poet brings out some of the prominent provinces of Uttara Pradesh like Koushambi, Kampilya, Hastinapura, Sravasthi, Kapilavastu, Varanavatha, Kanyakubja and so on.

We know how the life of Buddha is historically connected with Kapilavastu, Hastinapura is connected with Pandavas, Varanavata has found expression in Bhattanarayana's Venisamhara as follows;

इन्द्रप्रस्थं वृकप्रस्थं जयन्तं वारणावतम्।
प्रयच्छ चतुरो ग्रामान् कंचिदेकं च प्रञ्चमम्॥

The Kampilya has found expression in Shudraka's Mricchakatika as राजा ब्रह्मदत्त: नगरं काम्पिल्यं and so on.

A FINE ALLITERATION

We have a fine narration of the goodness of the people of Uttara pradesh here;

यत्राध्यापि शिथिलता ऋतुस्वाताङ्गनाजनागुरू धूपवासकृपण बन्धेषु न सौहार्देषु, मलिनता ईषात्कलन्नेन्धन काष्ठसञ्चयोद्वमत्पारावत पक्षधूसर धूमबिम्बानवरत धूमायितग्राम ग्रामटिका वसथ महानसेषु न सत्पुरुषहृदयेषु, कैतवं ध्यूतादि दुर्व्यसनेषु न सम्बन्धेषु, कालुष्यं मृत्तैलप्रवर्तित शिखावलवर्तिका विरचित कज्जलाचल विटङ्केषु न मनस्सु, गार्द्धं निगमागम पुराणकाव्यनाटक प्रबन्धेषु, न काञ्चनविभवेषु, कार्पण्यं मयूरव्यंसकायमान वितयसमसमानविधौ नातिथ्येषु, मौनं विपश्चित्तल्लजाधिष्ठित गोष्ठी सन्दर्भेषु नानौचित्येषु, अनुरक्तचातुरक्षिकं प्रणयप्रसङ्गेषु न कलहेषु संदृश्यते।

The dirt was found only in the smoke which used to emanate from the burning of the wood in the kitchen and not in the hearts of the great men, treachery was found only in playing dice and not in the relationship of the people, people were involved in the scholarship of acquiring knowledge regarding the Vedas, Agamas, Puranas, Kavyas and Natakas and not in amassing wealth and so on.

This particular passage to some extent resembles the following passage of Bana's Kadambari wherein he is narrating the greatness of the hermitage of Jabali;

JABALI'S HERMITAGE

यत्र च मलिनता हविर्धूमेषु न चरितेषु, मुखरागः शुकेषु न कोशेषु, तीक्ष्णता कुशाग्रेषु न स्वभावेषु, चञ्चलता कदलीदलेषु न मनःसु, चक्षूरणः कोकिलेषु न परकलत्रेषु, कण्ठग्रहः कमण्डुलुषु न सुरतेषु, मेखलाबन्धी व्रतेषु नेर्ष्याकिलहेषु, स्तनस्पर्शी होमधेनुषु न कामिनीषु, पक्षपातः कृकवाकुषु न विध्याविवादेषु, भ्रान्तिः अनलप्रदक्षिणासु न शास्त्रार्थेषु, वस्त्रसंकीर्तनं दिव्यकथासु न तृष्णासु, गणना रूद्राक्ष वलयेषु न शरीरेषु, मुनिबालनाशः क्रतुदीक्षया न मृत्युना, रामानुरागो रामयणेन न यौवनेन, मुखभङ्गविकारो जरया न धनाभिमानेन।

And within that hermitage there was darkness in the smoke rising from sacrificial offerings, and not (wickedness) in the deeds (of its residents). There was redness of the mouth in parrots, but not (redness of the face) is (caused by) in (caused by) anger. There was sharpness in the tips (of the blades) of the Kusha grass, but not (harshness) in the tempers (of its occupants). There was tremulousness in the leaves of the plantain trees, but not (fickleness) in the minds (of its residents). There was redness of the eyes in the cuckoo birds, but not (lustful glances) towards the wives of others. There was seizing by the neck, of the water gourds, but not (embracing round the neck) in cohabitation. There was the tying of the waste band during (the observance of) vows, but not (the binding of the lover by his mistress with her girdle) in realous quarrels. There was the touching of the breasts in the case of the sacrificial cows (when they were milked), but not (embracing the bosom) of beautiful women. There was the shedding of the feather on the part of peacocks, but not (showing partiality) in learned discussions. There was walking around during circumambulations of the sacred fire, but not (doubts) as regards the interpretation of the Sastras. There was talk about the (demi gods called) Vasus in the course of legends concerning divine beings but not (speaking about money) in greed. There was counting by means of the rosaries of the Rudraksha beeds, but not (concern shown) towards the (physical bodies) bodies. There was cutting off of the hair of the sages, during the initiation for a sacrifice but not (loss of children of the sages) by death. There was love for Rama owing to (the study of) the epic Ramayana but not (love for women) produced by youth. There was the facial change, consisting of wrinkles wrongut by old age, but not consisting of frowns) produced by the pride of rich.

A FINE ALLITERATION

In continuation with the greatness of Uttar Pradesh, the gifted poet has brought out a charming alliteration;

रिङ्गत्तारङ्ग भङ्गीविरचित धवलक्षीरशय्याऽद्रिकन्या
स्फीता ब्रह्मद्रवाङ्गी तुहिनगिरिगृहं क्षालयन्ती सयत्नम्।

शैलाच्छैलं सरन्ती विधिलिपिकुटिला भागधेयं सृजन्ती
आत्मानं पम्फुलीति प्रचुरहितधिया यत्र जीयात्सदेशः॥

SCENIC BEAUTY OF PRAYAG

Prayag is one of the important cultural centres of Uttar Pradesh and hence the poet befittingly narrates the beauty of Prayag;

तस्यैवोत्तरप्रदेशस्य हृदयगह्वरे स्यन्दननिभो विराजते तीर्थपतिः प्रयागः यत्रादौ सृष्टिप्रपञ्चाय भगवता लीला पुरुषोत्तमेन महाविष्णुना समादिष्टो विरिञ्चिः, शक्त्यापादनाय दशाश्वमेधान् सम्पादयामस। आस्थालुजन प्रत्ययायेव यत्राद्यापि गङ्गायमुनयोः अन्तर्वेदिकां कृशानु-कुण्डीकृत्य पौरन्दर दिगुदञ्चन्तर तरुणारुण बिम्बमग्निपिण्डीकृत्य सिस्नाषुजन पापल्मष समुच्यंच हव्यीकृत्य, पवनान्दोलित अर्थैः निरन्तरालता रायथमण्डले सोद्धारप्रसरं समारोहन् धूमरागिरिवाधि सोमवत्यमावास्यं प्राभातिक माघमास मिहिकाघनान्धकारो वातावरणं व्याप्नोति।

In the heart of that Uttar Pradesh, shines PRAYAG the most celebrated pilgrim centres wherein at the time of the creation, the creator ordered Vishnu to do the Asvamedha sacrifice. Wherein even to this day the pious people take a holy dip in the meeting point of the Ganga and Yamuna on account of which all their sins will depart and hence has sanctified the whole place.

KALIDASA'S ASSOCIATION WITH PRAYAG

Next, we have a graphic description of the association of Kalidasa with the holy place-Prayag;

अनुरक्तोर्वशीको यत्रोपगङ्गं प्रतिष्ठातपुर्यां प्रशशास सुभगम्मन्य-नृपशेखर मणिमृगाङ्कपौत्रौ राजर्षैरैलेयः पुरुरवाः। प्रणयरसभराक्रान्त चित्तयोश्चान्द्रमस सहोदर सुरसिन्धु सैकतपुलिन कन्दर्प विहारविवर्धत

मनसिजरागयोः कामिनोस्तयोः लीलाविलास काकुस्थ केलाभिरत्रैव कृत्तकृत्यतामनायि कविकुलगुरूकालिदासोपवर्णितस्सुगाङ्गाख्यो राजप्रासादः। उर्वशीविरहानल दग्धमानसः पुरूखा यत्रोन्मदीभूय त्रिपथगातारिणं मल्लिकाक्षं दयितागति मलिम्लुचरमन्यमानो अनवरतं सोल्लुण्ठमुपालेभे।

It is here that on the banks of the river Ganga Puruavas who belonged to the family of Ila got attracted towards the heavenly damsel Urvashi which has found expression in the play Vikramorvashiyam from the pen of Kalidasa. Ultimately Pururavas who was separated from Urvashi and hence he was burnt with the agony of separation became mad here. Here, the learned poet has established the relationship of Kalidasa with Prayag by illustrating the incidents of Vikramorvashiyam for which the basis is Pururava-Urvashi conversational hymn found in Rigveda.

A CHARMING MALOPAMALANKARA

One can find a charming Malopamalankara in the following description of Prayag;

क्वचित्तपश्चर्येव सितजीवनप्रभा निरन्तरात्या च, क्वचिद्गायत्रीव प्रसहादृत घनकल्मषभरा सतताधिष्ठिता च, क्वचित् राजधानीवाध्याश्रित दुर्गप्राकारा समुच्छ्रित प्रशस्तिसभा च, क्वचिद् रामायणकथेव सिन्धुपुलिनविश्रान्त प्राभञ्जनिः, विनिर्मितसेतुप्रभा च, क्वचिद् वाराणसीव प्रतिवेशस्य शङ्गरमण्डपा, संघुष्टमंत्रा च, क्वचिज् ज्ञानसम्पदिव श्लथीकृत सच्चिदानन्दा, तिरस्कृत सुरेशा च, क्वचिद् विश्वविद्यालय समज्येव कृतार्थस्नातका, पुरस्कृतपरोहिता च, कृचिद् महाभारतकथेव भीम शकुनिदुर्योधनभीष्मा तटस्थयोगेश्वरा च, क्वचित् परम्परेव श्रद्धयाभिवंध्य च, निसर्गार्जुनाऽपि कृष्णमयी, कूलमर्यादिताऽपि कूलङ्कषा, गृहीत देवव्रताप्यभीष्मा, वसुनिधानमूलाऽपि सलिलमात्रवसु स्त्रिपथगा भागीरथी यं प्रयागं तीर्थपतिं विघत्ते।

At some places, it resembles the rigorous penance performed, in some other places, it has similarity with the divine Gayathri, in some other places, it appears like the entrance of the king's capital which will be surrounded by forts, in some other places, it reminds us of the incidents of Ramayana, in some other places, it reminds us of the Varanasi where we have the Shankara shrine, in some other places we have the University-the temple of learning from where the graduates pass out incessantly and still in some places, it has semblance with the characters of Mahabharata.

Here one gets reminded of the following Malopamalankara in Bana's Kadambari;

क्वचित्प्रलयवेलेव महावराहदंष्ट्रा, समुत्खात धरणिमण्डला, क्वचिद् दशमुखनगरीव चपलवानरवृन्द भज्यमानतुङ्गशलाकया, क्वचिदरनिर्वृत्त विवाहभूमिरिव, हरितकुश समित्कुसुमशमीपलाश-शोभिता, क्वचिदाद्रवृत्त मृगपतिनादभीतेव कण्टकिता, क्वचिन्मंत्रेण-कोकिल क्रचप्रलापिनी, क्वचिदुन्मत्तेव वायुवेगकृतचाल शब्दा' क्वचिद्वधावेवोन्मुक्ततालपत्रा, क्वचित्समर भूमिरिव शरशतनिचिता, क्वचिदमरपतितनुरिव नेत्रसहस्रसंकुला, क्वचिन्नारायणमूर्तिरिव तमाल-नीला, क्वचित्पार्थरथपताकेव वानराक्रान्ता, कृचिवनिपति द्वारभूमिरिव वेत्रलताशत दुष्प्रवेशा, क्वचिद्विराटनगरीव कीचकशतावृता, क्वचिदम्बर-श्रीरिव व्याधानुगम्यमान तरलतारकमृगा, क्वचिद्गृहीतव्रतेव दर्शभर्तीवर-जरावल्कल धारिणी विंध्याटवी नाम।

In some places, it looks like the time of Universal destruction, its patches of ground being torn up by huge boars with their tusks. In some places, it looks like the capital city (Lanka) of the ten faced Ravana, being full of Sala trees with branches broken by crowds of restless monkeys. In some places, it appears like a spot where a wedding has just taken place, being decked with green Kusha grass, holy fuel, flowers, and Shami leaves. In some places, it has thorns as though it was terrified by the roar of the defiant lions. In some places, it is noisy with the comings of swarms of cuckoos as though it were intoxicated. In some places, like the delirious is rustled with the trees of Sala-trees, owing to the force of the wind as though it were not on its senses. In some places, it sheds down the leaves of tala trees, like a widows tears. In some places, it is overgrown with hundreds of reeds, like a battlefield. In some places, it was full of thousands of Netra trees, like the body of Indra the lord of the Gods. In some places, it is dark with Tamala trees like the body of Vishnu. In some places, in is infested with monkey, like the flag on Arjuna's chariot. In some places, it is in accessible owing to hundreds of cane plants grown there, like the court yard of a king. In some places, it is overgrown with hundreds of bamboos, like the capital city of king Virata. In some places, it is full of deer having their eyeballs trembling as they are chased by hunters, like the Chitra grass, fibrous roots and barks like a woman who has taken the vow of ascetic life.

THE HERMITAGE OF BHARADHWAJA

Next, the learned poet pen pictures the pious hermitage of Bharadhwaja;

तस्मिन्नेवंगुणविशिष्टे प्रयागे विलसति राघवचरणधूलि पवित्रितोद्देशो महर्षिर्भारिद्वाजाश्रमः। यत्र दण्डकवन प्रविविक्षुः दाशरथिः ससहोदर सदयितश्च किंचित्कालपर्यन्तमध्युष्य मुनिवर्थमुखाम्भोज प्रकीर्ण निगमागम रहस्य पुष्पासव बिन्दून् निपीयात्मानं धन्यवदान्यतमं मेने। जनकराज नन्दिनी यत्र त्रिवेणीकाम्बुचये कृतावगाहना भगवतीं भागीरथि पतिदेवरसौख्यं ययाचे। यत्र च

कैकैयीसन्दीप्त राजगृहषड्यंत्र हुताशनोद्दाम ज्वालावलीढ़ जिजीविषः, शशविषाणीभूत पितृसौख्योऽजागलस्तनी भूतजननी वात्सल्यो गन्ध र्वनगरीभूतऽभिरामरधूत्तम बान्धवो माण्डवीवल्लभो भरतोऽग्रज दर्भ गहनकान्तारापदयोध्यानमनुनेतुं सपुरजनपरिजन सैन्यसामन्ता मान्यवर्ग संप्रस्थितः भरद्वाजाश्रमातिथिभूतः, अणिमामहिमाध्यष्टसिद्धि गर्वितेन महर्षिणा भारद्वाजेन राजोचितसपर्याभिः सहेलमेव यथेष्ठं सत्कृतः।

In the holy place of PRAYAG, there is the pious hermitage of Bharadhwaja which was made sanctified by the contact of Sri Rama who visited it. There Rama spent some days with his brother Lakshmana and wife Sita having got the blessings of the revered Bharadhwaja who was well versed in Vedas and Agamas. There is the revered river Bhagirathi, Sita prayed for the well being of her husband Rama here. It is here that Bharatha along with all the people tried to meet Rama with the intention of bringing him back to Ayodhya to accept the throne, where he was extended cordial welcome and hospitality by the revered sage Bharadhwaja who was endowed with the Astasiddhis like Anima and others for which we have a reference in Amarakosha;

अणिमा महिमा चैव गरिमा लघिमा तथा।
प्राप्तिः प्राकाम्यमीशत्वं वशित्वं चाष्टसिद्धयः॥

DEPICTION OF BHARADHWAJA ASHRAMA IN CHAMPU RAMAYANA

We can note in passing that, Bhoja also mentions the hermitage of Bharadhwaja in his Champu Ramayana as follows;

अन्येध्युः वन्येन पथा प्रयातास्ते प्रयागे प्रतायमान होमधूमप्राग्भारं भारद्वाजाश्रमं श्रयन्तश्चाभिवंध्य तममन्दहर्षं महर्षिमनेनादिष्टवर्त्मना

वैकर्तनीपुरोपाप्यवं त्लवेन वैणवेन निस्तीर्य शमधनजन सन्निधान शमितशास्त्र वातक्लसत्व चरित्रविचित्रं चित्रकूटाचलमभजन्।

Then the next day through the path of the forest, Rama, Lakshmana and Sita went to the hermitage of Bharadwaja which was situated in Prayag and which is enveloped with the sacrificial smoke where they offered respects to the revered Bharadhwaja who was filled with joy on seeing them and later having crossed Vaitartani they reached Chitrakoota.

PRAYAG IS SANGAM

Next, the poet proves that place is a meeting point in every respect;

सङ्गमधरित्रीयं समेषाम्। न केवलं त्रिवेणी जलान्येव प्रत्युतरूदमान्यव्यत्रैकीभूतानि। अभाजगाम धृतक्च्छपीमारिराधयिषुः कविकुलगुरूः कालिदासः प्रत्यक्षं च अक्षिलक्षीकृतवान् सितासिते मञ्जुतरङ्ग चामरे समुद्रपत्न्योः।

This is a holy meeting place for everyone. Not only the three rivers come together here, but even the minds of the people come close here. Kalidasa who witnessed this place was an eye witness to it.

KUMARILA BHATTA'S ASSOCIATION WITH PRAYAG

Next, Rajendra Mishra depicts the association of the great Mimamsa scholar Kumarila Bhatta with prayag;

सौगतोपाध्याय द्रोहस्फुरितहृदयो गृहीतकाशीविद्वत्सभानुदिष्ट गुरूद्रोहोपयुक्त दारूणप्रायश्चित्तः प्रविष्ट कराल तुषानलः अदग्धार्ध-संहननोमहामीमांसक आचार्यप्रवर कुमारिल भट्टः अत्रैव जाह्न-वीतरे त्रयीतेजोऽवदातनुं देशिकोत्तमं कालटेयक आदिशङ्करं

स्वशिष्यप्रवरमण्डनमिश्रं विजेन्तुं च आदिश्य स्वाशीर्वचनैस्तं प्रत्युद्गम्य ससुखं प्राणांस्तत्याज।

It was here on the banks of the river Ganga that the famous Mimamsa scholar Bhatta entered fire as a mark of remoarse as he had caused droha to his buddhist teacher and before has death he met the great Shankara who hailed from Kalati and told him to have intellectual argument with his dear student Mandana Mishra as he had come to the end of his life.

This particular instance could be seen in the work Shankara Digvijaya as well as the Sanskrit movie Shankaracharya directed by Sri.G.V.Iyer.

ASSOCIATION OF KALACHURI DYNASTY WITH PRAYAG

The revered Gangeyadeva-one of the greatest kings belonging to the dynasty of Kalachuris came to Prayag towards the evening of his life to offer worship to the divine Bhagirathi;

प्रतापास्ताचल शिखराधिरूढ़ः कलचुरीराजवंशोत्पन्नः भास्करो गांगेयदेवकर्णोऽपि वार्धक्ये पुण्यक्षेत्रे प्रयाग ऽव शरीरत्यागकामनया भगवतीं भागीरथीं सिषेवे।

Even in the Ayodhya Kanda of Champu Ramayana of Bhoja Sri Rama refers to Bhagirathi very reverentially as follows;

मेध्याश्वमार्ग परिमार्गण संभवस्य
दिव्यौषधि कपिलकोपमहाज्वरस्य।
तातानुतर्पण पचेलिम भागधेयां
भागीरथीं भगवतीं शरणं भजामः॥

ASSOCIATION OF CHAITANYA AND VALLABHA WITH PRAYAG

Even the great saints of India like Vallabha and Chaitanya stayed in a hermitage called Avil which is not very far off from the Sangam;

गङ्गायमुना सङ्गमास्थलान्नातिदूरे अविल्लनाम्नि
प्राक्तनाश्रमे गङ्गवामतद्रस्थे गौराङ्गमहाप्रभु
चैतन्यदेवो महाप्रभुणा वल्लभाचार्येण सार्धं
तास्ताः पुराणवार्ताः कीर्तयन् कंचित्कालमुवास।

Moghuls and their association with prayag and the relevency of the name Allahabad;

ततश्चोदयति लोदिशर्कि राजन्यकुलकैरव वनीसंकोच कारिणि मुगलवंशभास्करे हुमायूँसूनो जलालुद्दीनेत्यपर संज्ञे नवरत्नमाल्य सुमेरूकल्पे महामहिम्नि भारतधारावशी कुहृदये, सम्प्रात्य कतिपयमरुध राधीशसौहृदे शूणैक्यपक्षपातिनि, राजराजेऽकबरे तीर्थपतिः प्रयागोऽयं राजाननदृष्टाऽपि परं महिमानं दधे। सततविद्रोहपरायणं शाहंशाह-सिकन्दर लौदिनापि प्रसह्य कुब्जीकृतं क्षमं, भासुरशर्किशासन संरक्षितं शीराजे हिन्देत्यपरसंज्ञं जौनपुरसाम्राज्यं, नेदिष्ठ निमंत्रणै नियिन्तुं सम्राट् अकबरः कड़ोपाघ्वं सूबेत्याख्यं राज्यं भंक्त्वा अज्यप्रवर्तितं इहालीधर्मं प्रख्यापयितुकामः इलहाबादाभिधं नूतनं राज्यं निर्ममे।

Then emerge the dynasty of Lodhis. Then Jalaluddin the son of Humayun started his regime and after him his illustrious son Akbar succeeded him who was known for the recognition of merrits. He was successful against Sikandar Lodhi who later on vanquished kad ara and Subas and to proclaim the supremacy of the Islam religion found a new name to the place called Ilahabad.

GUPTAS AND THEIR ASSOCIATION WITH PRAYAG

Gupta dynasty's regime is known as the golden age, and among the Guptas the most illustrious ruler was Samudragupta whose victorious pillar inscription we have here which is better known as Allahabad pillar inscription which is also known as Harishena's Prashastikavya as seen in History.

कौशाम्बीतः समुद्रगुप्तविजयप्रशस्ति लेखालंकृतं महाकवि हरिषेणकमनीय कवित्वकाञ्चन निकषोपलभूतम्।

THE ILLUSTRIOUS AKSHAYA VATA

Next, Rajendra Mishra refers to the illustrious Akshayavata which is situated here. It may be noted here, that Rajendra Mishra's one of the collection of dramas Natya Panchamrutam published from Allahabad in the year 1977 December has been termed as Akshayavat Prakashan;

यत्राधुनापि नन्दनविपिने पारिजात इव बाणभट्टोप वर्णित विंध्याख्यां, पुराणशाल्मलिरिव, श्रीरङ्गस्थ जम्बुकेश्वरायतन प्राङ्गणे जम्बुरिव, बोधगयाक्षेत्रे बोधिवृक्ष इव, पुरीदेवालयाजिरे अभीष्टा-भिलाष सम्पादनोहः, अन्य न्यग्रोधतरुरिव, महावत्यां चन्देलयुद्ध भरोदलसमर्पित चण्डिकायतने प्रोत्तुङ्गबिल्वविटपीव, कलिकत्तास्थ वनस्पत्युपधाने विनष्टा प्रत्यभिज्ञानमूल शताधिक प्ररोह संवधित महाविस्तारः प्रख्यातवटवृक्ष इव, अम्बरीषदेशस्य केलिफोर्निया राज्ये अवस्थितो निखिलानेहासो बृहत्तमः पुराणतमः जनरलशर्मन् इत्याख्य महापादप इव पुराणवर्णितो राराज्यते अक्षयवटः।

Even to this day, this illustrious Banyan tree stands out as a living monument in prayag as though it is the parijatha tree in the heaven, or the shalmali tree as narrated in the description of Vindhayatavi in Bana's Kadambari or the Jambu tree which adores the

Jambukeshwara in the vicinity of the pilgrim centre Srirangam, or like the Bodhi tree situated in Bodh Gaya, or like the Bilwa tree situated in Mahavati, or like the huge Banyan tree which has widely spread out its branches found in the Calcutta gardens or like the big tree named as general Sharman situated in California in U.S.A.

Here one can note that Rajendra Mishra is a widely traveled person not only within the country but even outside India. The above illustration prove the point on hand convincingly.

Here, one is tempted to quote the Shalmali tree situated in Vindhyatavi as found expression in Bana's Kadambari;

तस्यैवं विधस्य पध्मसरसः पश्चिमेतीरे राघवशर प्रहारजर्जरित जीर्ण तालतरूखण्डस्य च समीपे दिग्गजकरदड़ानुकारिणा, जरदजगरेण सततभावेष्टितमूलतया, बद्धमहालवाल इव, तुङ्गस्कन्धाव लम्बिभिः अनिलवेल्लितैः अहिनिर्मोकैः धृतोत्तरीय इव, दिक्चक्रवाल परिमाणमिव गृह्यता भुवनान्तराल विप्रकीर्णेन शाखासंचयेन प्रलय-कालताण्डवप्रसारित भुजसहस्रमुडुपति शकलशेखरमिव विड़ंबयितुमुद्यतः पुराणतया पतनभयादिव गगनस्कन्धालग्नः निखिलशरीर-व्यापिनीभिः अतिदूरोन्नताभिः जीवितया शिखाभिरिव कण्टकैराचिततनुः इतस्ततः परिपीत सागर सलिलैः गणनागतैः पत्ररथैरिव शाखान्तरेषु निलीयमानैः क्षणमम्बुभरालसैः आर्द्रीकृतपल्लवैः, जलधरपटलैः अत्यदृष्टशिखरदेशः। तुङ्गतया नन्दनवनश्रियमिव अवलोकयितुमभ्युध्यतः, समीपवर्तिनामुपरि संचरतो गगनचलगमन खेदायासितानां रविरथ-तुरङ्गमाणां सृक्कपरिसृतैः फेनपटलैः संदेहिततूलराशिभिः, धवलीकृत शिखरशाखः, वनगजकपोल कण्डूयन लग्नमदानिली न मत्तपस्या-यिनामूलेन समुपगत, कोटराभ्यन्तर निविष्टैः, स्फुरद्भिः सजीव इव मधुकरपटलैः दुर्योधन इवोपलक्षित शकुनिपक्षपातो नलिननाभ

इव वनमालोपगूढ़ो नवजलधरव्यूह इव नभसि दर्शितोन्नतिरखिल भुवनतलावलोकन प्रसाद इव वनदेवतानामधिपतिरिव, दण्डकारण्यस्य नायक इव, सर्ववनस्पतीनां सखेव, विंध्यस्य शाखाबाहुभिः उपग्रह्येव विंध्याटवीभवस्थितो महाजीर्णः शाल्मलीवृक्षः।

And on the western shore of that lotus lake which is of the described kind, and near the group of those seven ancient Tala trees, which had been pierced formerly by the fall of Rama's arrows, there is a big, old shalmali tree, It is possessed as it were, a large watering basin built around its root, since it was always encircled by an old python resembling the large long trunk of a quarter elephant. It appears to be wearing an upper garment, as it were, reason of the sloughs of snakes, which are tossed to and fro by the wind.

On account of its numerous branches which spread out in all the spaces of the world and which seem to be taking the measure of all the ten quarters, the tree appears as if it were trying to imitate the god Siva who wears the crescent moon for his tiara, when he spreads out his thousand arrows during his violant dance at the time of world destruction. It rests on the shoulders of the sky, as if out of fear of falling down on account of its being very old. It is surrounded by creepers going round its entire body and are very permanently visible. Its trunk is studded with projection thorns as though they were the moles spotting the body in old age. The region of the top is not seen even by the masses of clouds, which like birds risen to the sky from various quarters after having drunk the water of the ocean and being heavily laden with water, rest for a moment in the spaces between its branches, and wet its foliage with their water. On account of its extreme height the tree appears as though it were trying to gaze at the beauty of Nandana garden in heaven. The branches of its top are whitened by the clusters of coffin which are compounded by the beholders with flakes of foam falling from the corners of the mouth of the Sun's chariot horses fatigued by the labour of going through the sky, and coursing just above it and at no great distance. It has a root capable of lasting to the end of the world, which on account of the rows of intoxicated bees lying upon the ichor sticking to it owing to its being robbed against by wild elephants with their temples, appears to be indeliably fixed as it were by being fastened down with steel chains. It pulsates with life as it were by reason of the swarms of bees entering into, and governing around its hallows. Like Duryodhana it has flappings of the wings of birds visible (on its branches etc) like Vishnu (the lotus navelled god) it encircles by rows of thickets. Like a bank of new clouds, it raises its height in the sky. It is as though it were a palace from which the sylvan deities might look at the surface of the entire earth. It is as though the head chief of all the trees. It is as if it were the bosom friend of the Vindhya mountain. And it stands up, embracing as it were the body in the form of the Vindhya forest, with its branches serving as arms.

TULSIDAS AND HIS ASSOCIATION WITH PRAYAG

As though to continue the tradition of the revered Yagnavalkya and Bharadhwaja and the Valmiki, Goswami Tulsidas spent some time in Revered Prayag when he was on his pilgrim, tour;

महर्षियाज्ञवल्क्य भारद्वाजप्रवर्तित ज्ञानसत्रापकृत तापत्रयेऽक्षुण्ण-

ज्ञानविज्ञान कथाप्रसङ्ग इव, रघुनाथ यशोगाथा मानस विहरणोत्सुको, दयिताभिव्यक्त मर्मच्छिदुक्ति प्रहरणोधृत मोहान्धकारानिला विलोचनो अभिनववाल्मीकिः गोस्वामी तुलसीदासोऽपि तीर्थयात्रक्रमे कंचित्कालं निनाय।

UNIVERSITY OF ALLAHABAD

Next, Rajendra Mishra vividly portray the greatness of the University of Allahabad which has already celebrated its centenary celebration as could be noticed in another work of Rajendra Mishra written in the year 1987 when the centenary celebrations were held and the work is entitled as Shatabdhi Kavyam where in we can find a beautiful Virodhabhasalankara;

यत्र च भारतभुवि स्थिरतामुपगते साम्राज्ञी विक्टोरिया साम्राज्ये ब्रिटिशशासकैः जगत्प्रथितः प्राच्यकेंब्रिजेत्यपरनामा महान् विश्वविद्यालयः १८८७ तमे क्रिस्ताब्दे सितम्बरमासस्य त्रयोविंशतिततमतारीकायां संस्थापितः अधीति बोधाचरण प्रचारणमयेन विद्यावयव चतुष्टयमहिम्ना चतुर्मखन्वं दधदिव विशाल धारकियंत्रं मोहनिद्रासुप्तान् विधार्थिजनान् प्रतिहोरमुद्बोधयत्येव कर्णविवख्यापिना मधुमधुरनिनादैः। अधीतयजुर्वेदा अप्यौत्तरीयाः, कण्ठस्थीकृतशारीरिकभाष्या अप्यवेदान्तिनः परिशीलित काव्यशास्त्रा अप्यधाविनः, आकण्ठनिपीतकाव्य नवरसकापि शायनीका अप्यप्रमत्ताः, परिसमाप्तदशरूपका अप्यधानंजयाः विव्रतावलोकाप्यधानिकाः, शकुन्तलास्यलावण्यसौजन्यादि प्रशंसका अप्यदुष्यन्त, वनेचरावेदित सपत्नवैभवोद्विग्न द्रौपध्युद्गारोपशिक्षिता अप्ययुधिष्ठिराः, संहष्ट पञ्चसन्धि प्रकरणा अप्यदृष्टसवर्णवृद्धिप्रसङ्गाः, परिशीलित प्रत्यया अप्यकृदन्ताः, अतद्धिता क्रियायुक्ता अपि संशयितोपसर्गाः, देववाणीसमर्चको विध्यार्थिनो यत्र स्वगुण महिम्ना अध्यापि प्रभवन्ति।

Queen Victoria in the year 1887 September 23rd established the University of Allahabad which is known as the Eastern Cambridge. There are four wall clocks which have been put on all the four directions which make the sleeping students alert and reminds them about their daily routine. Here the poet introduces a nice Virodhabhasalankara regarding the scholarship of the students. They have memorised the entire Vedanta Sutras of Badarayana, they are not Philosophers. Though they have gone through Kavyas, and Sastras they are not scholars. Though they have enjoyed the nine Rasas present in Kavya, they are not intoxicated with it, though they have enjoyed the charm of Shakuntala, they are not Dushyantas, though they are conversant with the story of Mahabharatha they are not Yudhisthiras, though they have studied the entire Samasa, they are not acquainted with the Bahuvrihi, though they have been taught the Sandhi portion, they cannot distinguish the Savarna, Guna and Vriddhi Sandhis. Though they have been taught pratyayas they do not have the knowledge of Kridantas. The students of Sanskrit still flourish in this University even to this day. The above Virodhabhasalankara could be taken in the sense of mockery also if we take into account the fall in the standards of students.

HOLY DIP AT PRAYAG

Next, Rajendra Mishra reminds us of the tradition of Prayag. Every year during the auspicious time of Maghamasa, People come in leaps and bounds to take bath in this holy Prayag to cleanse them with sins. We come to know from the travelogue of the Chinese traveller Huien Tsang that even Harsha the great had come to this place and taken a holy dip;

समागत उाव माघमासे प्रतिहायनं यत्र स्वर्धुनी परिपूत

जलस्नानार्थिनां दिग्दिगन्तागतसाधुभक्तानां महान्सम्मर्दो जायते। प्राग्तनीयं परम्परा। निखिलो नरपथ प्रशस्ता वर्धानवंशावतंसो महाराजाधिराजो हर्षदेवोऽपि प्रयणस्नानपर्वणि समागत्य शरीर स्वस्तवर्ज्यं यावदुपस्थितं सर्वमपि वस्त्रान्तर रजतकांचनमणि भूमि ग्रामादि वसुजातं सत्पात्रेभ्यः प्रदाय परां प्रीतिमुपजगामेति ज्ञायते चीनयात्रिणो ह्वेनसांगस्य विवरणैः।

THE MAHAKUMBHA CEREMONY

Next, Rajendra Mishra vividly portrays the Mahakumbha ceremony which is held once in twelve years;

ततश्च प्रतिद्वादशवर्षं समायाति महाकुम्भभिधं पर्व यस्मिन् सर्वेऽपि महामण्डलेश्वराः शंकररामानुज माध्वनिम्बार्क वल्लभाचार्य चैतन्य सम्प्रदायवन्तः अन्येव सर्वतंत्र स्वतंत्राः तपस्विनो निरञ्जन-निवर्णिोपासीनादि दशनाममार्गदीक्षिताः साधवश्च महद्भिः सम्भारैः समागत्य मासं यावदध्युष्य गङ्गायमुनयोः अन्तर्वेध्यां कृतार्थतामनुभवन्ति।

Then for every twelve years Mahakumbha ceremony is held where in all the Mahamandaleswaras belonging to the sects of the followers of Shankara, Ramanuja, Madhwa, Nimbarka, Vallabha, CHAITANYA and other saints come to this place and stay here for a month and get the blessings.

PRAYAG-THE PILGRIM OF THE PILGRIM CENTRES

Next, the poet comes to his conclusion that Prayag is really the pilgrim of the pilgrim centres where in he sums up all his earlier views;

प्रयागस्तीर्थपतिः यामुनगाङ्गसङ्गम क्षेत्रत्वात्, विरिञ्चि सम्पादित दशाश्वमेघाध्वरं भूमित्वात्, अक्षयवरालं कृतत्वात्, शेलेयोर्वशी प्रणयविवाहोद्देशत्वात्, कालिदासशंकर कुमारिल चैतन्य वल्लभरूप-सनातन तुलसी मकूलदास साधुना बिन्दुत्वात्, भारद्वाजाश्रम गौरवत्वात्,

समुद्रगृप्तप्रशस्ति निधान भूतत्वात्, शहीदे साजभेत्याख्य चन्द्रशेखर प्राणेत्सर्गक्षेत्रत्वात्। स्वातंत्रसमरकेन्द्रालयानन्द भवनवैशध्यात्, मदनमोहन-मोतीलाल जवाहरलाल बहादुर, सप्रूबन्धु कैलाशनाथेन्दिरा प्रभृति राष्ट्रभक्तानां गङ्गानाथामरनाथादि प्रख्यातविदुषां निरालापन्त महादेवी रामकुमारादि सिद्धलेखकीनां, कर्मभूमित्वाद् विशिष्यते महाकुम्भपर्व-स्थलेभ्यो अन्येभ्यः। १९८९ मिति खिस्ताब्देऽस्मिन् महाकुम्भपर्वेदं फरवरीमासस्य षष्ठतारीकायां सम्पन्नं जातमिति सुविदिततरं समेषां यस्मिन् सार्धैककोटिमिता हिन्दवो गंगाभक्ताश्च पूतगाङ्ग जलाभिषेकैः मोक्षसहोदरं सौख्यमवापुः। चरमो महाकुम्भोत्सव आसीत् विंशति-शताब्दाः।

Prayag is really the pilgrim of the pilgrim centres because it is the meeting point of the sacred Ganga and Yamuna, because the creator had initiated the Asvamedha sacrifice here. It is adored by the great Akshayavata, it is connected with the romantic episodes of Pururavas and Urvashi, it was auspious because people like Kalidasa, Shankara, Kumarila, Chaitanya, Vallabha, Tulsidas, Malukdas and others visited it, Bharadhwaja Hermitage is located here, which was sanctified by Sri Rama who visited it during his fourteen years of an ascetic life. It was the central point at the time of the freedom movement as the greatest of the political leaders like Madana Mohana Malaviya, Motilal Nehru, Jawahar lal Nehru, Lal Bahadur Sastry, Sapru, Indira Gandhi and others were associated with it. Great intellectual savants like Ganganatha Jha, Amarnath and others were associated with it. Some of the great writers like Panth, Mahadevi, Ramkumari were connected with it. In the year 1989 in the month of February sixth, Mahakumbha took place wherein one and a half crores of Hindus were supposed to have taken a holy dip here which is the last mahakumbha ceremony for the twentieth century.

Rajendra Mishra concludes his Teertha raja Champu with the following statement wherein the title of the work is mentioned;

भारतं देवलोकोऽसौ संस्कृतं देवभारती।
तीर्थराजोऽपि वैकुण्ठो मोक्षो गङ्गावगाहनम्।

Bharatha is Devaloka and Sanskrit is the language of Bharatha, Prayag is Vaikunta and invoking the blessings of Ganga is salvation. The following stanza of Shankara also subscribes to the latter half of the above statement;

भगवद्गीताकिंचिदधीता गङ्गाजललवकणिकापीता।
सकृदपि येन मुरारिसमर्चा क्रियते तस्य यमेन न चर्चा॥

To conclude one can say that this Teertharaja Champu of Rajendra Mishra is like a source book on Prayag which narrates all the important places and people associated with it like the scenic beauty of Prayag association of Kalidasa, Madan Mohana Malaviya, Motilal Nahru, Jawaharlal Nahru, Indira Gandhi, Lal Bahadur Shastri, Ganganatha Jha, Kumarila Bhatta, Chaitanya, Vallabha, Panth, Mahadevi, Ramkumari and others.

The serene hermitage of Bharadhwaja narrated here reminds us of Rama's association with prayag in Ramayana. Some of the illustrious dynasties which were associated with Prayag like the Guptas, Kalachuris, Moghuls, Loudhis, the illustrious Akshayavata, the University of Allahabad which is known as the oriental cambridge, the Mahakumbha ceremony and others have all been pen pictured here. From the point of view of the style, some of the prose passages here remind us of Bana's style. Rajendra Mishra's wide travel and personal visit to all the holy places of India comes through very effectively in some of the illustrations he has made. All the descriptions are realistic and not imaginary because he is a witness to it and he is the son of the soil of Allahabad and hence the descriptions are bound to be authentic. Some of the Alankaras like Upama, Malopama, Utpreksha, Anuprasa, and Virodhabhasa have been appropriately introduced at the right places and it has added beauty to the work.

Perhaps one can sum up this assessment on Teertharaja Champu in the words of Bhaskaracharya Tripathi the editor of the Sanskrit Journal Doorva from Madhya Pradesh in has introduction to the Vidyottama Natika of Rajendra Meshra;

दिव्या वाणी वलितमधुरा स्वर्धुनी भूतलेऽस्मिन्
हिन्दी भाषा नवलकलयापावनी भानुकन्या।
अन्तर्नीरं प्रवहति च या रागरम्या कविश्री
रूत्सङ्गेताः सुखयति समं तीर्थराजोऽभिराजः॥

8

ASMAT CHAMPU-AREYAR SRIRAMA SHARMA

Asmat Champu is an un-published work based on Visistadvaita system of Philosophy propounded by Ramanujacharya and written by Vidvan.Areyar Sri Rama Sharma-Principal, Government Sanskrit College Melukote-Karnataka in the year 1965. It is unfortunate that this work has not seen the light of the day even after three decades. The work is divided into five chapters and each chapter has been named as Varnaka. The five Varnakas are अमृतकिरणोदय:, स्थानसम्प्राप्ति:, मतिविलास:, अद्भुतयोग: and तत्वांशदर्शनम् There are eighteen subjects dealt with in the first chapter such as मङ्गलम्, कैरतिनीक्षेत्रे पंचदैवतवर्णनम्, आधुनिक लोकिवृत्तम्, ग्रामास्थिति:, नगरस्थिति:, नागरिकयुवक्रलम्, सज्जनस्थिति:, वेंकटार्यवर्णनम्, रामप्रतिष्ठार्थ यात्रा, नगरवर्णनम्, जलाशयं, षण्ड्वनम्, सागर:, महेन्द्रगिरि:, मार्गप्रदेशा:, सूर्यास्तम् and चन्द्रकलोदय:।

Thus in the first chapter itself, most of the characteristics of the traditional Mahakavyas are fulfilled.

In the second chapter called स्थानसम्प्राप्ति the main subjects are

रसिकसंवाद,:, द्रविड़देशविजय:, राहुकाल:, तार्किकविषय: चाटु:, हास्यरसविचार:, अन्धकाखर्णनम्, तैलशकटगमनम्, नेल्लूरून-गरम्, रङ्गनाथवर्णनम्, पिनाकिनीनदी, निद्रितजनवर्णनम्, निद्रावैभवम्, मार्गप्रदेशादि:। सूर्योदय:, सूर्यस्तुति:, मार्गगमनम् शार्दूलतटाकाग्राम-प्रदेश:।

The third chapter deals with रामप्रतिष्ठा, पूर्वरङ्ग:, यज्ञवार वर्णनम्, वेदपारायणदिवर्णनम्, भोजनवर्णनम्, काफीवैभैवम्, वीरभारताभिप्राय:, शमविरोधिनी हास्यकथा, शमप्रधानसज्जनचरितम्, श्रीवैष्णवसिद्धान्त संग्रह:, प्रमाणप्रमेयस्थानम्, काव्यस्वरूपदर्शनिम्, पद्यविमर्श:, समस्यास्वारस्यम्।

The fourth chapter narrates ग्रामसङ्गीतगेयपद्यानि, कृष्णगीतम्, लक्ष्मीगीतम्, वीरनृसिंहगीतम्, अर्चावतारविचार:, श्रीरामप्रतिष्ठा प्रकरणम्, तदीयाराधनदेवोत्सव:, देवस्तुति:, उत्सवेश:, दिव्यपुरुषदर्शनम्, तत्क्षेत्रे कामसान्निद्यम्, व्याघ्रमुनिचरितम्, व्याघ्रेभ्य: उपदेश:, शेषनाग वर्णनम्, अर्जुनगिरौ व्याघ्रचरितम्, नागार्जुनयो श्चरितम्, व्याघ्राणां परिनिर्वाणम्।

The last chapter depicts प्रतिष्ठाशेष:, यांत्रिकप्रत्यागमनम्, नदीतटम्, सहस्रनामवैभवम्, मद्रनगरप्राप्नि:, कैरविणीपार्थसारथि वर्णनम्, सिद्धान्तसार:, गुरूपरंपरानुसंधानम्, गुरूवैभवम्, षब्द्धब्दपूर्त्यु-त्सव संग्रह:, वन्दनमालिका, मङ्गलम्, चम्पूविमर्श:, कविपरिचय:, ग्रन्थकरणसमय:, ग्रन्थशरीरसंस्थानम्, उपकार स्मरणम्, समर्पणम्, ग्रन्थपल्लव:, कवि नामाक्षरस्तहस्त:, प्रतिकृतिलेखनकाल:।

Thus there are ninty topics dealt with in this champu and here an attempt is made to highlight some of the topics as a sample survey in the form of evaluation of the work.

The following Mangala sloka has a fine alliteration;

श्रीरङ्गमङ्गलमणिं करूणानिवासं
श्रीवेंकटाद्रि शिरवरालय कालमेघम्।

श्री हस्तिशैल शिखरोज्वल पारिजातम्
श्रीशं नमामि शिरसा यदुशैलदापम्॥

Under आधुनिकलोकवृत्तम् the author describes how people have lost all their morality these days with pain in his heart;

न वा यक्षसूत्रं नवा ब्रह्मसूत्रं
न वा शब्दसूत्रं न कट्यंगसूत्रम्
न वा नीतिसूत्रं न राष्ट्रं सुसूत्रम्
न सूत्रं प्रजानां विसूत्रं विसूत्रम्॥

There is neither sacrificial thread nor Brahmasutra. Neither an order in speech, nor a thread tied round the waist. Neither the people have a thread to move forward and everywhere the continuity has been broken.

A NICE PARADOX

One can notice a fine paradox in the following stanza;

यत्र गौः पूजिता तत्र पूज्या शुनी
यत्र वा ब्राह्मणाः तत्र पाषण्डिनः
यत्र वाप्यार्यता तत्र हा कलेच्छता
यत्र वा भारताः तत्र हा दूरताः॥

Where cow was revered now the dog is revered, where Brahmins were honoured there wicked people are honoured. Where Aryans had an important place, there the foreigners are now, where people had love for the country, that has been lost now.

शब्दचमत्कार

The demoralising condition of the modern day world is nicely depicted in the following prose passage;

मानवानां मानवत्वमेव नष्टं, दैवतं पुनराप्तुं
कष्टम्, दानवत्वमुपेक्षमपि दुष्टं, समाविष्टं
भ्रष्टमदृष्टं, दृष्टमतीवक्लिष्टं, किं भविष्यतीत्यस्पष्टं
हन्तमहत्कष्टम्।

Now there is no humanity in people. It is difficult to get back divinity, though we want to avoid bad elements, it will cling to us. What we are seeing is terrible and what will happen in future is difficult to predict. Oh, it is terrible.

A NICE PARODY

The famous stanza

मनोजवं मारुततुल्यवेगं
जितेन्द्रियं बुद्धिमतां वरिष्ठम्
वातात्मजं वानरयूथमुख्यम्
श्रीरामदूतं मनसा स्मरामि

has been parodied as

मनोभवं मारुततुल्यवेगं
जितेन्द्रियं बुद्धिमतां वरिष्ठम्।
वागात्मजं कानरयूथमुख्यम्
श्रीकामदूतं शिरसा नमन्ति॥

ADOPTION OF SUBHASHITA

The famous Subhashita

शैले शैले न मणिक्यं
मौक्तिकं न गजे गजे
साधवो नहि सर्वत्र
चन्दनं न वने वने॥

has been adopted here as न जले जले मौक्तिकम, न खनौ खनौ कनकम्

NICE ALTERATION

We can note a nice alliteration in the following stanza;

धर्मप्रतिष्ठापन कर्मसिध्यै
शर्मप्रदोवोऽस्तु स वासुदेवः।
वर्मापि वज्रोपममस्तु गुप्त्यै
कर्मस्सतां धर्मनिधिं तमेव॥

SECOND CHAPTER

The logicians have been made fun of here;

तार्किककुमतिः, स खलु स्वयं पचति। प्रातः पाकारभ्य रात्रावेव अर्धपाकः, पादपाको वा भवति। तस्य परिकरा डाव यथा–

धूममहानसवह्नि कसूलैः
आर्द्रककण्ठस्थलि प्रचारकैः।
भ्रष्टतिलैर्धरपिठरीपाकैः
रात्रिचरः किल तार्किकसूदः॥

This evil logician cooks. If he commences cooking in the morning by the time it is night he would have completed half or quarter. His ingredients are smoke, Kitchen, Fire and so on.

हास्यरसविचारः

We have an admirable portrayal of हास्यरस here;

हन्त! रसेषु किल नवस्वपि हास ऽवासौ परम रमणीयः सर्वसुलभश्च। आबालवृद्धं च वयः परिपाकमन्तरा स्त्रीप्रविभागमवधूय सोऽयं निर्विशेष ऽको रस्यमानो रसो नाम हासः।

न हासयति यश्चैव यश्च नैव हसत्यपि उभावपि सुखस्थाने निस्सुखौ प्रस्तराविव। हासोद्धानन्दनिस्यन्दः सर्वव्यापी समीकरणः विद्वद्विलसितोल्लासः केन बद्धुं स शक्यते॥

Indeed of all the nine Rasas, हास is the best and easily accessible one. The only Rasa which could be enjoyed by all-whether one is young or old, man or woman is Hasa.

One who never laughs and one who never allows others to laugh, both of them will be devoid of pleasures.

Hasa is like a wind is all pervasive. Who can ever avoid it as if it has its sway even among the scholars.

निद्रावैभव

We have a graphic description here about the sleep;

हन्त! निद्रा नाम केवा न मोहयति।
चराचरगुरूः भगवानेव दिव्यशेषशायी
तस्या अवशोऽपि वाशश्वावलक्ष्यते।

Oh whom will not this sleep take into its fold? Even the God who is the creator also is not devoid of Sleep.

मालोपमा

How different people sleep in different postures is graphically portrayed here with a nice मालोपमा which reminds us of the अन्तःपुर of Ravana wherein women were sleeping as depicted in Sundarakanda of Valmiki Ramayana.

अत्र कश्चिन्मत्स्य इव निर्निमिषलोचनः, निद्राह्रदावगाढ़श्च, कश्चित्कूर्म इव निगूहितकरचरणेन्द्रियः, कश्चिद्वराह इव घर्घरश्वासः, कश्चिनृसिंह इव व्यात्ताननः। कश्चिद्वामनइव कुब्जीकृत स्वचरणः, कशितत्परशुराम इव राजमशकद्वेषी, तृणीकृतस्वर्ग सौख्यश्च। कश्चित्कमललोहित विलोचनः, श्रीराम इव कश्चिद्बलभद्र इव वारुणी मदाधिक तंद्रालुः। कश्चित् कृष्ण इव शेषभागेऽपि शयालुः। बुद्ध इव कश्चिन्निरस्त बाह्यविषय शून्यवादमनुप्रविष्ट इव कश्चिज्जिन

इव गलिताम्बरः। कश्चित्कलिखि जितकलिः प्रशान्तकोलाहलः कश्चिद्बलभद्र स्वप्नतुरगारूढ़श्च क्वचित्प्रजापतिरिव जड़ः, शम्भुरिव कश्चिद्विरुपाक्षः। कशिचिदर्धनिद्रा नारीश्वरश्चेति।

Some appeared like a Fish by opening and closing their eyes, some others had folded their hands and legs in their sleep and thus appeared as though they were like Tortoises, some were snoring and making noise like Swinė in their sleep. Some were sleeping with their hair spread over and thus resembled Lord Narasimha. Some appeared like Vamana as they had contracted their body and some were stretching their legs gradually and thus appeared like Trivikrama. Some appeared as though they had abandoned even the heavenly pleasures and some of them had broad beautiful eyes and thus resembled Sri Rama. Some had abandoned their senses from the external things and thus appeared like Buddha (Here one can note Sri Rama Sharma's prowess over Buddhism). Some had abondoned their clothes and thus appeared like Jina. Some appeared as though they have established their victory over Kali age and thus appeared like Kalki. Still some others were quietly sleeping. वेदाभ्यास जड़: Some others were dreaming, some were motionless like Parajapati or Brahma in their sleep. This reminds us of Kalidasa's statement. Some were partially sleeping and hence they appeared to be Siva the odd eyed one.

The above prose passage nicely narrates Dashavatara concept in the pretext of sleep.

How the sleep is the best tonic for the healthy body is portrayed here next; निद्रा नराणां वपुषः परमारोग्यपोषिणी।

THIRD CHAPTER

The first stanza of this chapter has a beautiful alliteration;

भगवत्पादुकाद्वन्द्वं भूत्वा भुवनमङ्गलम्।
भरतं भावयन्तोऽमी भुजैर्भागवता विभुः॥

पूर्वाचार्यपरम्परा

The tradition of the Visistadvaita system has been portrayed in the following stanza;

कुलशेखर यामुनमुनि
काञ्चीपूर्णा लक्ष्मणमुनीन्द्रम्।
करेश भट्ट वरद
व्यास प्रमुखान्नुमस्सह स्तुतिभिः॥

Let us offer our salutations to our noble ancestors like Kulasekhara, Yamuna, Kanchipoorna, Lakshmana Muni, Vyasa and others.

रूपक

One can notice a beautiful रूपक here;

तत्र त तेषां जाठरवैश्वानर पूर्णाहुतिप्रदानाय करा इव स्रुवः, कदलीदल विशालखण्डमेव चारुपत्रं, भोज्यानि च हव्यानि, भथयाणि च समिधः, लेह्यानि च पृषदाज्यानि, चोष्णाचित प्रोक्षणोप स्पर्शन प्रणयनजलानि, करकरायमाणा जिह्वा इव ज्वलनज्वालाः, विवृत-वदनान्येव होमकुण्डानि, कूर्चव्यंजनान्येव दर्भसंस्काराः॥

At the time of their जाठरवैश्वानर the स्रुव served as hands, bananas served as charu vessel, the different Bhojyas are Havyas, the Bhakshyas were Samits, the Lehyas were Ajya, the water was chosya, the tongue oozing out from the mouth was like the tongue of fire. This reminds us of the seven tongues of fire as narrated in Mundakopanishad.

Next the author picturesquely portrays how the cooks led the visitors;

शीघ्रमेहि, आनयपुनरानय, परिवेषय परिवेषय, पुनः पुनः

पृच्छा, किमिष्टं? किं परिवेषयाणि? भक्षय भो भक्षय, पिबत हे पिबत, खादत खादत, मोदत मोदत, किं ददानि? लज्जा विमुच्यताम्, यथेष्टं पृच्छताम्, यथेच्छं भुज्यताम्।

Come fast, bring bring, serve,serve. Ask again and again, What do you Like? What shall I serve? Please eat, eat. Please drink, drink. Please be happy. What Shall I Give? Don't be Bashful. Feel free and ask.

काफीवैभवम्

The काफीवैभवम् portrayed here has a fine sense of humour;

कालकूटाच्च पीयूषादादायैकैकमक्षरम्
कापीं चतुर्मखश्चक्रे चतुरां वर्णसंकरात्।
गोष्ठी नवामृतरसः षडतीतपाकः
लोकाधिकप्रचुर ञष रसो हि काफीः॥
सौहार्दबन्धन विधेरयमेकतन्तुः
सम्बन्धितोषण विधे सरसोपहारः।
वागीशाद्या सुमनसः सर्वार्थानामुपक्रमे
यं पीत्वा कृतकृत्यास्युः तं नमामि कफेश्वरम्।
गायत्री चैव सावित्री त्वमेवासि सरस्वती
काफि त्रिसंध्यां त्वां सेवे सर्वकालं प्रसीदतः।
काफीति मातृकावर्ण द्वयमंत्रमयामिमाम्।
भाषार्थबन्धरां वन्दे सर्व विद्यार्थिसेविताम्॥

Having taken the first letter from कालकूट ie का and पीयूष nectar the creator has created the word coffee which is the best example for mixture.

This is the nectar which is being served in all the seminars which excel the six fold drinks and it is a well known Rasa called coffee.

This is the drink which unites people and strengtness their friendship to last longer.

I bow down to the revered Coffee by consuming which the gods like Vagisha and others achieved everything in their lives.

Oh coffee, I adore you thrice a day like while performing Sandhya people adore Gayathri, Savithri, and Saraswathi. May you be favourable to me at all times to come.

This word coffee which has two varnas in it is the favourite drink of the students also.

The crux of Srivaishnavism is nicely brought out in the following passage;

सर्वे वेदाः प्रमाणं तदनुगुणगणं सात्त्विकं सारशास्त्रं
श्रीमन्नारायणाख्यं चिदचिदनुगतं सुद्गुणं शेषितत्वम्।
भक्तिर्मुक्तेरुपायः प्रपदनमपि तत्सर्वसत्वाधिकार्यं
भक्तिर्लोके परस्मिन् परमजनमिति श्रीमतं वैष्णवानाम्॥

All the Vedas are valid means of knowledge and all the Sastras which are in keeping with orthodoxy are also Pramana. Here the highest principle is Narayana who is the combination of Chit and Achit who is endowed with all the auspicious qualities in him and he himself is the principle of Seshi. The means for salvation is Bhakti or Prapatti (self surrender to god) and salvation is always otherworldly विदेहमुक्ति and not जीवनमुक्ति (Here it should be noted that the Visitadvaitins do not accept Jeevan Mukti as accepted by Advaitins).

Contribution of Ramanuja to this system of philosophy is highlighted next;

वेदान्तभूमिं विषयांविधिज्ञैः
समीकृतां सम्यगधीत्य पूर्वम्।

श्रीभाष्यवेदिं परिकल्प्य तत्र
श्रुतप्रकाशादि शुभप्रबन्धैः॥
सुवर्णरत्नं द्रमिड़श्रुतीनां
भाष्यं च सिंहासन मारचय्य
चतूरहस्य प्रवरोक्त भाष्य
स्तमैतिदंघ्रि सुदृढ़ विधाय॥

Having established the doctrine of Sri Vaishnavism on a firm footing, having composed Sri Bhasya on the Brahma Sutras as well as the works like Sruta Prakashika and then after Rahasya Trayasara and others he became immortal.

The various theories of poetics like Rasa, Dhwani, Vakrokti, Auchitya, etc have been dealt with at length next.

FOURTH CHAPTER

Yugmaka could be noted in the आदिपाद and अंत्यपाद of the following stanza;

काण्डं काण्डं टकटक इति भ्रामयन्तस्साघातं
नारनाचारी चतुरचरणाः चक्रयूथे युवानः।
भासागीत चयगतपदं तोटकाद्यैस्सनालं
गायं गायं सरसहसितं गोकुलं स्मारयन्ति॥

A fine अंत्यप्रास could be seen in the following stanza;

किन्नसुखं! वद मानसकाये
इदमिति न किमपि पापनिकाये
नरकपतनमाये काये
किन्न सुखं वद मानव काये॥

The following prose impresses us with the letters having अनुप्रास :

ऽवं बहिरपि नटविटगायक, वादक, वाग्जीवक, खेलक, संवादक, परिहासक, परिवादक, जालक, मौहूर्तिक, यक्षोरगगणान्तश्च, याजक, निर्वाहक, पाठक, परिचारक, जापक, संवेषक, पेषक, परिपालक, पूजक, परिगायक, याचक, परिदायक, वैदिक, जन प्रतिष्ठेत्सव दिनानि चत्वार्यभूवन्।

पदप्रास could be noted here;

मंत्रं मन्ता मंत्रगो मंत्रमंत्र्यो
मंत्रांगोऽयं मंत्रणं मंत्रगम्यः।
मंत्रार्थोऽयं मंत्रमंत्रार्थदोऽयं
मंत्री मंत्रान् मंत्रयेन्नः सुमंत्रान्॥

A fine Yugmaka is presented to us here;

वीरथ्यां वीथ्यां भोजनायोपविष्टाः
पात्रं पात्रं स्वांकऽवदधानाः।
भोजं भोजं भोज्यराशिं कराभ्यां
तोषं तोषं नोत्थितुं पारयन्ति॥

From the point of view of analysing the style of the poet the following stanza could be taken as a representative;

राम! राम! रमणीयनाम! ते
नाम नामासुरसायनं पिबन्
काम काम कमनीय काय! ते
काय कायमिह कामये विभो॥

A FINE PARADOY

The Bhagavad Gita Stanza

यस्मान्नोद्विजते लोको लोकान्नोद्विजते च यः

could be seen here as

येन नोद्विजते लोकः लोकान्नोद्विजते च यः।
स द्विजः प्ररुषव्याघ्रः स ऽव भगवत्प्रियः॥

A FINE मालोपमा

We have a fine मालोपमा in the following passage;

महानागः प्रकुपितः प्रमत्त इव महागजः, प्रोद्धोदित इव गृहसिंहः। प्रस्फुरित इव भस्मान्तर ज्वलनः। प्रस्फुरित इव शतहनीगोलः, प्रोच्चलिनोघ इव महानदः

and so on.

FIFTH CHAPTER

One can note a nice alliteration in the following prose;

देवानामपि देवतं, प्ररुषाणासपि च पुरुषोत्तमः, स्त्रीणामपि स्त्रीवरः, जड़ानामपि जड़ः, योगिनामपि योगेश्वरः, सकलजनमनोनुभाव मनुवर्तमान इव सर्वमनुगृण्हन् पापान्यपि धुवानः, पावनान्यपि पुनानः, कनकमणिमुक्तामुख निखिलरत्नमय कल्पतरूकल्प कमनीय काय प्रालम्बित पल्लवप्रलय मनोहरणनिपुण चरण शरणीयः शरणमस्मदादीनाम्।

Here we have a beautiful character sketch of Krishna who as god of gods, greatest among people, more feminine than the females, in active among the inactives, Yogin among the Yogins, blessing everyone in keeping with their mentalities, the remover of the wicked, the protector of the good, May our head be under his feet.

The prowess of Venkatacharya over different systems of philosophy is depicted next;

ञवमिहाधुना सम्प्रदायसम्यक् निर्वाहकाचार्यैः श्रीमदुभयवेदान्त निष्णातैः, देशीयवरदाचार्यवर्यैः, समुन्मीलित ज्ञानलोचनरसो प्रवर्तनाचार्यः वेंकटार्यो विराजत। यश्च उभयवेदान्तवेत्ता सरहस्य संस्कृतद्राविड़ वेदान्तवेदयिता निरतिशयज्ञानभक्ति वैराग्यविनातिशय विभूषणः, साहसिकसरसवचनमात्र वशीकृत सफलजनहृदयः, न

केवलं वचनगुणैः अपितु अनवद्यैरात्मगुणैः अस्मानाह्लादयति। यस्य श्री रामायण भारत भागवत भगवद्गीता प्रबन्धविस्तर श्रीभाष्य विष्णुसहस्रनामभाष्य दिव्यप्रबन्धभाष्य रहस्यत्रय वचनभूषणाचार्य हृदयरहस्यत्रयसार तत्तद् व्याख्यानविमलः सकल दिव्यसूरि प्रवचनैः प्रतिध्वन्यमानमिव भगवद्भागवताचार्य भक्ति भरभरितं आनन्दसागर-निमग्नमिव प्रतिकलमाचक्षते।।

Like this he was an adept in Ubhaya Vedanta, an opener of the divine vision known as Sri Venkatacharya. He was an expert in Vedanta an embodiment of Jnana, Vairagya, Humility, who was not only impressive through his knowledge but also through his conduct. He was like a mirror to the knowledge of Ramayana, Mahabharatha, Bhagavatha, Bhagavadgita, Sribhasya, Vishnu Sahasranama Bhasya, Divya Prabandha Bhasya, Rahasya Trayasara, Divyasuri Prabandhas and so on.

Next the Vaishnava Sampradaya is enumerated with a fine आदिप्रासः

जयति यदुगिरिगिरौ नृसिंहः
जयति यतीन्द्रसुतोप्यथो यतीन्द्रः।
जयति गुरूपरम्परा पवित्रा
जयति च वैष्णवसूरि सम्प्रदायः।।

Lord Narasimha shines on top of the hill Yadugiri whereas Yatindra also shines. The unbroken tradition of the saints shines and the tradition of Vaishnavism continues.

We have an account of कविपरम्परा in the end;

आस्ते यदुगिरिर्नाम देशे कर्णाटिके गिरिः।
यत्र नारायणश्रीमान् सिंहसिंहाननौ हरिः।।
सदा तदीय सेवैक फलास्वाद रथोत्सवाः।
विलसन्ति बुधास्तत्र शास्त्रसर्वस्ववासवाः।।

तेषां विनयविद्यादि गुणैर्गुरुतरोर्गुरूः।
वेंकटार्य इति श्रीमानासीत् कविकुलांकरः॥
बालधन्विकुलोद्भूत शिङ्गरार्यतनूभवः।
सांख्ययोग रहस्यार्थ वेदान्त द्वयवेदिनः॥
तस्यैव दुहितुः पुत्रः पुत्रवत्तेन पालितः।
ज्ञानविज्ञानसम्पत्तिं प्रापितश्चास्ति बालकः॥
तेन रामाभिधानेन कवितोल्लासमैतुकात्।
नित्यशिष्येण विदुषां आस्मच्चम्पूरकारिशम्॥

In the state of Karnataka there is a place called Yadugiri (Melukote) wherein Narayana the Lord has stationed himself.

Every year Rathotsava and other festivities are celebrated to that God in a grand scale. (Vairamudi Festival wherein the diamond studded crown is offered to God).

There was a noble person endowed with humility and knowledge by name Venkatarya.

He was born in the illustrious family of Baladhanvis (to which Jaggu Vakulabhushana also belonged) and was the son of Singararya who was a master of Sankhya, Yoga, Rahasya Traya and Ubhaya Vedanta. (Sanskrit as well as Tamil).

I am his grandson and he had treated me like his own son and educated me under his personal care.

My name is Rama and I am desirous of writing poetry and with the help of my scholarly students I could compose the work Asmat Champu.

To conclude, one can say that Asmat Champu is a harmonious blend of Tradition, Philosophy, Humour and History. The work speaks about the caliber of the poet who can blend the traditional thoughts in a modern outlook. काफीवैभवम् and निद्रावैभवम् have a fine touch of humour. Some of the Alankaras like उपमा, अनुप्रास, रूपक, युग्मक, etc have been used very forcefully here whether it is a prose or a poetry. At the end one only hopes that this work gets published in near future and earns its due place among the post independence Champus.